Bold Girls

A play

Rona Munro

Samuel French - London
New York - Toronto - Hollywood

BOLD GIRLS

Commissioned by 7:84 Scottish People's Theatre and first performed at Cumbernauld Theatre, Strathclyde, on September 27th, 1990 with the following cast of characters.

Deirdre	Andrea Irvine
Marie	Paula Hamilton
Nora	Joyce McBrinn
Cassie	Julia Dearden

Directed by Lynne Parker
Designed by Geoff Rose

Subsequently presented in London at Hampstead Theatre on 4th September, 1991, with the following cast:

Deirdre	Catherine Cusack
Marie	Orla Charlton
Nora	Britta Smith
Cassie	Imelda Staunton

Directed by John Dove
Designed by Robert Jones

Synopsis of Scenes

Scene 1   Marie's house. Late afternoon

Scene 2   The Club. That evening.

Scene 3   Outside the Club. Later that evening

Scene 4   Marie's house. Later that night

The play is set in West Belfast

Time: the present

For Pat

AUTHOR'S NOTE

My starting point was simply to write a play about women's lives in the North of Ireland. What I eventually wrote was a play about four very particular women in West Belfast and it was the product of a lot of laughs, a lot of whiskey and a score of stories. I'd worked in and visited Belfast on and off over five years. When I visited the areas of town that are really touched by war I stayed with families doing what families do anywhere in the world.

I don't think the battles women fight or the daily struggles they have are different to those in any other area with bad housing or high unemployment except that guns make a difference to everything. But this isn't a story about guns. It's the story of four bold women.

Rona Munro

Bold Girls was joint winner of the Susan Smith Blackburn Award for the best play by a woman in the English-speaking world, 1991. Rona Munro received the Evening Standard's Most Promising Playwright Award 1991 for *Bold Girls*.

Scene 1

Marie's house. Belfast. Late afternoon. Present day

It is irons and ironing boards and piles of clothes waiting to be smoothed, socks and pegs and damp sheets waiting for a break in the Belfast drizzle for the line; it's toys in pieces and toys that are just cardboard boxes and toys that are new and gleaming and flashing with lights and have swallowed up the year's savings. It's pots and pans and steam and the kettle always hot for tea; it's furniture that's bald with age and a hearth in front of the coal fire that's gleaming clean

At the moment it's empty, an unnatural, expectant emptiness that suggests this room is never deserted; it's too stuffed with human bits and pieces, all the clutter of housework and life

There is a small picture of the Virgin on one wall, a large grainy blow-up photo of a smiling young man on the other. He has a seventies' haircut and moustache

Deirdre is not in this room, she's crouching on all fours on her own talking out of darkness in which only her face is visible. She is wary, young

Deirdre (*moving from all fours*) The sun is going down behind the hills, the sky is grey. There's hills at the back there, green. I can't hardly see them because the stones between here and there are grey, the street is grey. Somewhere a bird is singing and falling in the sky. I hear the ice cream van and the traffic and the helicopter overhead.

Black-out; after a few minutes Lights come up on Marie's house

Marie bursts into the room with her arms laden with four packets of crisps, two of Silk Cut and a packet of chocolate biscuits. She is cheerful, efficient, young. She drops one of the crisps, tuts in exasperation, and looks at it

Marie (*shouting back out the door*) Mickey! Mickey were you wanting smoky bacon? ... Well this is salt and vinegar ... Well, why did you not say? Away you and swap this ... Catch now. (*She hurls the bag*) No you cannot ... No ... because you'll not eat your tea if you do! (*At the doorway*) Mickey, pick up those crisps and don't be so bold.

Marie comes back into the room and starts two jobs simultaneously. First she puts the crisps etc. away, then she fills a pan with water and throws it on the stove. She starts sorting her dry washing into what needs ironing and what doesn't; she sorts a few items then starts peeling potatoes; all her movements have a frenetic efficiency

Nora enters with a pile of damp sheets. She is down-to-earth, middle-aged

Nora Is that the last of them, Marie?

Marie Just the towels . . . Oh Nora, you didn't need to carry that over, wee Michael was coming to get them.

Nora Och you're all right. These towels is it?

Marie That's them.

Nora This'll need to be the last. I've a load of my own to get in.

Marie Oh here Nora, leave them then!

Nora No, no, we're best all getting our wash done while it's dry. We'll wait long enough to see the sun again.

Cassie sticks her head round the door. She is Nora's daughter, sceptical, sharp-tongued

Cassie Can I ask you a personal question, Marie?

Nora Have you left that machine on, Cassie?

Cassie Do you have a pair of red knickers?

Marie I think I do, yes.

Cassie With wee black cats, with wee balloons coming out their mouths saying "Hug me, I'm cuddly"?

Marie (*stops peeling potatoes briefly; giving Cassie a severe look*) They were in a pack of three for ninety-nine pence.

Nora You see if you leave it, it just boils over, you know that Cassie.

Cassie And did you put those knickers in the wash you just gave my mother?

Nora It's because that powder isn't really biological, it's something else altogether.

Marie What's happened to them?

Nora I think it's for dishwashers. But it was in bulk, cheap you know? I got a load of it at the club last month, awful nice young man, do you know that Dooley boy?

Cassie And did my mummy just drop those bright red knickers with their wee cats, right in the middle of the road, right by the ice cream van, as she was coming across from our house to yours?

Nora Did I what?

Marie Oh *no*! (*She increases the pace of her peeling*)

Nora Cassie, will you get back over the road and see to that machine before the foam's coming down the step to greet us.

Marie Where are they?

Cassie At the top of the lamp-post. I didn't know wee Colm could climb like that, he's only nine.

Nora Och I'll do it myself. (*She moves to exit with a heap of towels*)

Marie Hold on Nora, I'm coming too.

Cassie I wouldn't. After what's been said about those knickers I'd just leave them alone, pretend you never saw them in your life.

Nora All my lino's curled after the last time. I'll never find a colour like that again.

Nora exits

Cassie And did you know your wee Michael's just swapped a packet of salt and vinegar crips for a wee plastic cup full of raspberry ice cream syrup?

Marie (*erupting towards the door*) MICKEY!
Cassie I'll get him. (*Calling off*) Mickey, come here . . . 'Cause I want you.

Cassie exits

Marie finishes the potatoes and dives into the ironing again

Marie He doesn't just drink it, he wears the stuff.
Cassie (*off*) Give me that cup now.
Marie In his hair and everything.
Cassie (*off*) Because it's poison.
Marie Then he won't eat his tea and what he does eat comes straight back up again.
Cassie (*off*) I am an expert in poison, a world expert, and I'm telling you that stuff will kill you. I do know. I took a G.C.S.E. in identifying poisons.
Marie Threw his hamburger clear across the room last time. Frightened the life out of his Aunty Brenda.
Cassie (*off*) It gets your intestines and eats them away till they just shrivel up like worms. It's worse than whisky.
Marie I wouldn't mind but he doesn't even like the taste, he just likes being sick.
Cassie (*off*) I'll tell you what happens to all those men that drink whisky and all those wee boys that drink raspberry ice cream syrup; their intestines get eaten away and their stomachs get eaten away and all the other bits inside just shrivel up and die. Then they've got no insides left at all and all they can do is sit in front of the television all day and cough and shout for cups and cups and cups of tea because that's the only thing that can fill up their awful, empty, shrivelled insides . . . Yes just like him . . . and him as well, so will you give me that cup? That's a good boy.

Cassie enters the room with a plastic cup of red syrup

Marie Your tea's on the table in half an hour, Michael.
Cassie (*to Michael*) What? (*To Marie*) Can he still have his crisps.
Marie (*wavering*) Och . . .
Cassie No. Best let the poison drip its way through your intestines as fast as possible. Crisps would clog it up. (*She moves into the room; takes a swig of the syrup*) Put some vodka in that and it would make a great cocktail.
Marie Do you want a beer? I've cans in.
Cassie No, I'll wait a while. Are you still on for the club tonight?
Marie Oh . . . Well . . .
Cassie Marie!
Marie I've no one to watch the kids.
Cassie I thought Brenda was coming in?
Marie She said she'd try but I think her John's out tonight.
Cassie When is he not? Well we'll take Mickey and Brendan down to hers before we go.
Marie Och . . .
Cassie What?

Marie I've nothing to wear.
Cassie What about your red dress?
Marie I've nothing to go with it.
Cassie What about your cuddly kitten knickers? Look, when did you last
have a night out?
Marie I was over at yours watching that video just the night before last.
Cassie Oh, it'll take you a while to get over the excitement of that, I can see.
Marie Well it cost me a bit of sleep Cassie, that film.

Nora enters with a fabric sample in her pocket

Nora Marie I need your mop. What did I tell you, Cassie?
Cassie Sure it was only a film. Nothing real to it at all was there, Mummy?

Marie fetches the mop·

Nora Foam right up the walls.
Cassie You know that video we saw with Marie, *The Accused*, remember?
Her winning the court case and all, who could believe that?
Nora I came in the kitchen and all the stuff out the bin was floating around
on top of it, a packet of fags bobbing out the door——
Cassie Oh not my *fags*.

Cassie grabs the mop and exits

Nora settles herself down

Nora She was no good, that girl, if you ask me.
Marie Who?
Nora Jodie Foster or whatever you call her. I'm not saying she deserved it,
mind, but she should've known better, she should've known what'd be
coming to her.
Marie But was that not the thing of it Nora, that no woman deserves——
Nora (*interrupting*) Och she should've learnt better at her age. What do you
think of that?

Nora hands Marie the fabric sample

The colour of it, what do you reckon to the colour? It's unusual isn't it?
Unusual. Different. I don't think I've ever seen the like of that.
Marie It's lovely.
Nora So it is, and it's a good heavy fabric you see, you could do your
curtains in that and your loose covers.
Marie You could.
Nora Well I'm getting the end of a roll of that; fifteen yards of remnant and
that'll be my front room just a wee dream again.
Marie That'll be some price will it not?
Nora Oh I've a deal worked out with your man at the club, it won't be shop
prices he'll be charging. Anyway, they won't cut off the electric or the gas
this month and we must be due some summer by next month and who
knows if I'll live longer than that, so I'll be all right for a while, and I'll
have my room the way I want it.

Marie (*handing it back*) It is a nice bit of cloth.
Nora (*stroking it*) Just feels rich doesn't it? So are you coming out with us
tonight, Marie?

Cassie sweeps back in, brandishing the mop and a packet of soggy cigarettes

Cassie A wee bit of foam just dripping over the top! I thought I'd need my
aqualung the way you were talking.
Nora I hope you didn't let it drip on my good lino!
Cassie And what I'd like to know is, if everything in the kitchen was bone
dry, how was it my fags were sopping wet on top of the machine?
Nora Sure it wasn't me that put them there.
Cassie Sure it wasn't you puffed that packet down to two and them too
damp to light at all now.
Nora Och you're killing yourself with those.
Cassie And what are *you* doing? Bit of interior decor? Tar-filled lungs: what
the best dressed bodies are wearing.
Nora To say nothing of the money you're burning up.
Cassie Oh they're a terrible price, you're right there, just as well you've
mine to puff on. Here Marie, put these under the grill for me will you?

*Cassie hands Marie the soggy cigarettes. Marie takes them and then offers
both Cassie and Nora out of her own pack*

Nora Thanks Marie. (*To Cassie*) Our Martin never grudged me a cigarette.
Cassie That's because our Martin smoked mine as well.
Nora You! You'd grudge a dry hand to a drowning man.
Marie Maybe I will come out tonight.
Cassie There's no maybe about it.
Nora Are you not coming out with us, Marie?
Cassie Yes she is.
Marie I just don't know if I can get a sitter.
Nora Sure, put Brendan and wee Michael over with our two. Our Danny's
watching all of them.
Cassie Well our Danny's watching *Nightmare on Elm Street 365*, but I
daresay that'll keep him awake long enough to notice if they try and run
away from home.
Marie Well . . .
Nora I know how you feel love, but you can't mourn forever.
Cassie Who's mourning?
Nora Cassie!
Cassie Michael's been dead three and a half years, Mummy. I should think
she could try a wee smile on for size now and then don't you? Sure he was
hardly here when he was alive.
Nora God forgive you, Cassie.
Cassie And who was that came out with us last month drank a pint and a
half of vodka and tried to climb into the taxi driver's lap on the way home
to show him how to change gear?
Marie (*laughing*) Well he was in second, the eejit, the whole way.

Cassie Was that Michael Donnelly's mourning wee widow carrying on like that or was I hallucinating?

Nora God forgive me for bringing a child into this world with a heart of flint and a tongue to match.

Nora exits

Cassie Heart like a Brillo pad, that's me. That was B.T.'s taxi by the way; it was broke.

Marie (*sitting down*) Was it? Why did he not say?

Cassie (*sitting down*) I think he tried but you were too busy trying to remember all the words of *Life in the Fast Lane*. Then he couldn't breathe too well by then either, not with you squashing him into the steering wheel like that.

Marie Cassie! You should've stopped me!

Cassie There was no stopping you, Marie. B.T.'s never been able to get it past first since.

Marie I don't remember any of it, you know.

Cassie Just as well. So why won't you come out?

Marie Have you fallen out with your mummy?

Cassie I fell out with my mummy on the delivery room floor. Why won't you come out, Marie?

Marie Och, I've things to do here.

Cassie (*looking round*) Looks great to me. Want me to help you dust the lightbulbs?

Marie I just need a bit of quiet, time on my own.

Cassie Well you're in the wrong house for that.

Marie No, sometimes I get a sit to myself, by the fire, when the kids are in bed.

Cassie And what do you do?

Marie I just wait.

Cassie Wait for what?

Marie (*hesitating*) Cassie—do you believe in ghosts?

Cassie stares at her for a minute, then casts a quick nervous glance at the photograph on the wall

Cassie Has he been back? Have you seen him?

Marie No, not Michael. It's a wee girl, all in white.

Cassie A wee girl?

Marie nods

Well, who is it?

Marie I don't know.

Cassie Well, who does it look like?

Marie She looks like Michael.

Cassie Sacred Heart!

Marie You know how me and Michael always wanted a wee girl.

Cassie I remember.

Marie Then other times—she looks like me.

Cassie But—you're not dead.

Marie Well, you remember that dress I was married in, that wee white mini-dress?

Cassie nods

Then when Michael brought me here—I'd never seen it. Even on my wedding day I still thought we were moving into his parents' back room—then he brought me here, asked me how I liked our wee home—and I just stood at the end of the path there and stared . . .

Cassie Yes?

Marie That's where she stands. And stares.

Cassie Oh Marie!

Marie (*laughing*) So am I cracking up at last, Cassie?

Cassie I think you should get out of this house and get a good stiff drink or twelve down you.

Marie (*laughing*) I think you're maybe right.

There is the sound of a distant explosion. Both stop for a moment. They don't appear unduly alarmed

Cassie What side was that from?

Marie Sounded like it was down the front somewhere.

Cassie Sounded like it was a good way from here.

Marie Och, it's time I was getting the kids in anyway.

Marie wipes her hand and exits

(*Off; calling*) Mickey! Brendan! That's your tea ready.

Cassie gets up slowly, looking after Marie. She hesitates a second, then moving fast she goes to the photograph of Michael senior on the wall. She scrabbles down her front and pulls out a wad of money; she conceals it behind the picture. She straightens the picture again, steps back, then turns. She freezes in shock, staring out the window

Nora enters. She now has a towel round her head

Nora There's buses burning all the way up the Falls.

Cassie (*distracted*) What?

Nora (*looking to the window*) What is it?

Marie enters

Marie That's the Brits coming up the road. Close that blind, will you Nora?

Nora moves to do so

(*Talking to her kids off*) All right, you can have it in your room, but don't you be dropping chips on those clean downie covers.

Nora (*peering round the edge of the blind as she closes it*) Ahh! Will you look at what those great boots are doing to my nasturtiums!

Marie (*to Cassie*) Brendan got one of those computer games for his birthday, can hardly drag the pair of them out of there now. (*She puts food on plates*)

Nora I've only got two feet of garden, you'd think they could walk round it.

Marie He had it in here but I couldn't take the noise, so then he shifted it through; he'll sit through there in front of it even when he can see his breath and he's got to wear gloves to punch the wee buttons. Did you hear that Brenda's got a heater in every room in her house there? I says Brenda, if you switch them all on they'll be bringing you the bill by parcel post. Just steams the damp out anyway; it's like a Turkish Baths in her front room. Are you OK, Cassie?

Nora (*turning*) The only flowers in the whole road and they have to go and jump on them . . . Are you OK, Cassie?

Cassie Sure, why wouldn't I be OK? So what's happening?

Nora There's buses burning all along the Falls.

Marie exits with two plates of food

Cassie What?

Nora There's one just outside the supermarket there and there's a great lot of smoke further back as you look along the road.

Cassie Well, what's that for?

Nora Sure it doesn't have to be for anything does it?

Cassie Well, what's the date?

Nora No there's no anniversaries or nothing. I was just asking your wee woman there, we couldn't think of anything.

Marie enters

Marie They're saying there's shooting on the main road.

Cassie Who's shooting?

Nora No one seems to have a clue, but there's a road block going up the top of the road there.

Cassie Well, we thought we heard something going up down the front there didn't we Marie?

Marie Put the radio on. There'll maybe be something in a minute.

The Lights change. Spotlight on Deirdre

Deirdre (*speaking from her own space*) It's raining. The sky is grey. There's a helicopter up there, in the sky. I can hear it. It watching. It's raining on the shops. On the smoke, on the kids. It'll come in round the windows, it'll beat in the doors, can't keep it out. I'm wet, I'm cold. I want to get inside. There's burning, making the sky black. The sky's full of rain and the sound of the helicopter. I want to get inside. Can't keep me out.

Fade Light on Deirdre. Lights up on Marie

Marie It was a terrible wet day when I got married. A wet grey day in nineteen seventy-four and I couldn't get to the church for the road blocks. I was standing out on my step there with my mummy screaming at me to come before I got my good white dress dirty from the rain—only I was wetter from crying than the clouds could make me, because Michael Donnelly was the only boy I'd ever wanted for myself and me just seventeen. He was the only boy I'd wanted at all and it was still a miracle to me he wanted me back—but then since I've always had to work hardest at believing miracles and anyway I knew they only fell in the laps of the pure in heart, now it seemed certain to me that a pile of Brits and a road block would lose me Michael altogether—for why would he wait an hour or more at the church, when he'd that smile on him that made you feel wicked and glad about it and that look to him that caught your eye when he was walking down the street. Just with the way he put his feet down, bold and happy together, and those hands that were so warm and gentle you hardly worried where he was putting them and why would a man like that wait two hours in a cold church for a wee girl in a damp wedding dress? (*Pause*) And my mummy's trying to pull my daddy in 'cause he's shouting at the Brits saying this was the greatest day of his daughter's life and hadn't they just spoiled it altogether? Then this big Saracen's pulled up and they've all jumped out and my mummy's just going to scream when do they not offer us an escort through the road block? So that was my bridal car to the wedding, a big Saracen full of Brits all grinning and offering us fags and pleased as punch with themselves for the favour they were doing us. I hardly dared look at them. I was certain the big hulk sitting next to me was one of them that had lifted Michael just the year before but oh they were nice as anything. There was wanted men at the wedding and everything. Sure I'd grey hairs before I was ever married. And then I was married and Michael brought me here and the rain stopped; it even looked like the sun had come out and I stared and stared, just standing at the top of the path in my wee white dress that was still half soaked. It felt like we'd won through everything, the weather and the road blocks and the Brits and there were never going to be bad times again—because I was never going to be without him again. Well—I was just seventeen after all.

The Lights revert to normal

Nora "Reports of disturbances in the west of the city"? As if we hadn't noticed. Can I borrow your hair-dryer Marie?
Marie Sure help yourself, it's just by my bed there.

Nora moves to leave

Nora Well, it looks like none of us will be getting out tonight.
Cassie Why not?
Nora You'll not get a taxi down this street tonight, Cassie.
Cassie They'll be gone before you've your face on Mummy, with the time you take.
Nora Well I hope you're right. Our Danny won't get home from his work.

Nora exits

Marie Our Brenda's probably stuck in town as well.
Cassie Well, what's it all for; that's what I want to know?
Marie Someone'll know. Here, I'll get you some dinner, Cassie.
Cassie No, no, you're all right.
Marie Come on, I've it all ready here.

Cassie No, no, we've a meal ready for us across the street; we were just waiting on Danny. I gave my crowd theirs before I came out.

Marie Will they be all right?

Cassie Eileen's over there, her telly's been lifted.

Marie They never came to her house?

Cassie They did, half the street out watching them stagger out the door with it, took her video as well. She said she didn't mind the publicity but she was half way through watching *Home and Away* and they wouldn't even wait till she saw if they caught those two in bed or not . . . No but I'm on a diet.

Marie A diet! What for?

Cassie To lose weight!

Marie That's what I mean. What for?

Cassie Have you ever seen me in a bikini, Marie?

Marie I have not and I shouldn't think anyone else will either unless you were planning on sunbathing on that wee tuft of grass your mummy calls a lawn, or unless you've got some toyboy hidden away just waiting to sweep you off to Spain.

Cassie Well when I meet him, Marie, I want to have the figure for it. Anyway I've got this calorie chart, so all I can have today is half a grapefruit.

Marie Half a grapefruit? What kind of diet is that?

Cassie You have to weigh it up, a little of this or a lot of that. Do you know how many calories there are in a gin and lime? And I'm only allowed one thousand three hundred a day so if I'm wanting a drink tonight that's all I get to eat.

Marie That can't be healthy, Cassie.

Cassie Sure it is, you balance it out over the week. Fruit juice and yoghurt all day tomorrow.

Marie And ten gin and limes and a half a grapefruit today?

Cassie *Six* gin and limes, I worked it out . . . mind you, I could always give the grapefruit a miss couldn't I?

Marie Cassie, that can't be healthy at all——

There is the sound of a few gunshots; they sound close at hand

Marie and Cassie freeze for a second

Marie That was at the back of us, wasn't it?

Cassie nods

Marie goes to peek out past the edge of the blind

Cassie Must be something big.

Marie looks carefully up and down the street

Anything?

Marie (*shaking her head; still looking out*) So why don't you try that BBC diet? Brenda lost ten pounds with that.

Cassie I want something quick. You wait, Marie, I'll have a completely new body by the end of the month.
Marie Whose will you have?

There is a thunderous knocking at the front door

Both Cassie and Marie stare at each other, terrified

Cassie Sacred Heart!

Marie runs to the door to the hall

Marie (*shouting off*) Mickey, Brendan, you stay in that room! (*She waits there, just looking at Cassie*)

There is more knocking at the front door

Nora catapults into the room with her hair half dried

Nora (*frightened*) That's someone at your door Marie.

Marie moves over to peer round the blind again

Marie I can't see the step from here.
Cassie Just leave it Marie.
Marie Sure if it was anybody to worry about they'd've had the door in by now anyway. (*She hesitates looking towards the hall*)
Cassie Just *leave* it, Marie.
Marie Maybe it's someone needing to go through to the back.
Cassie And they wouldn't be knocking either, it'd be excuse me Mrs and straight through your kitchen with the Brits on their heels.

Marie starts to move towards the door

Marie I'll keep the chain on the door.
Cassie *Marie!*
Marie You stay here.

  Marie exits

Nora (*crossing herself*) Mother of God, did you hear those shots?

Cassie nods

They wait, watching the door

  Deirdre comes into the room. She looks about fifteen but could be younger or older, she's wearing a white mini-dress, damp and grubby, battered white trainers on her feet. Her legs are bare and scratched, there are more scratches on her arms. She has heavy black make-up on, smudged slightly around her eyes as if she's been crying. She stands uncertain in the centre of the room

  Marie enters behind her

The three older women just stare at Deirdre

Deirdre Can I stay here till I'm dry, Mrs? They won't let me up the road.

There is a pause then Marie finally stirs

Marie You better sit down by the fire (*She switches on the TV*)

Deirdre sits by the fire

Nora, Marie and Cassie slowly sit as well, watching her

Nora I don't know your face.

Deirdre says nothing. She doesn't look up from the fire

 Well where are you from?

Deirdre jerks her head without turning

 Where?

Deirdre (*sullen, quietly*) Back of the school there.

Nora What's that?

Deirdre (*loudly*) Back of the school there.

Nora Those houses next the off-licence?

Deirdre nods

 I know where you are. So what happened to you then?

Deirdre shrugs. She looks up and catches Cassie's eye

Cassie turns quickly to look at the TV

Marie Will you take a cup of tea, love?

Deirdre nods

Marie goes to make it

Nora stares at Deirdre a while longer, then turns to Cassie

Nora So Cassie, looks like that wee brother of yours will miss his tea altogether.

Cassie (*with her eyes on the TV*) Looks like he might.

Nora I hope he's the sense to stay in town.

Cassie Sure he'll phone next door, let us know what's happening.

Nora Aye he's a good boy.

There is a pause while everyone watches the TV in an uncomfortable silence

Marie brings Deirdre the tea and some biscuits. Deirdre takes it without saying anything, starts to eat and drink furtively and ravenously. Cassie and Marie exchange glances over her head

Marie Turn the sound up on that will you, Nora?

Nora turns the sound up

Cassie Is that *Blind Date*?

Nora You should know, you've been sitting here staring at it.

Cassie Will you look at what that woman's wearing!

Nora What's wrong with it?

Cassie She looks like she's ready to go in the oven for Christmas dinner.
Nora I like Cilla Black, she'd a great singing voice.
Cassie Pity she hasn't the dress sense to match.

Another pause. All of them including Deirdre keep their eyes fixed on the screen

Marie (*turning to Deirdre*) Have I not seen you around here before?

Deirdre shakes her head

(*Certain*) I thought I had.
Cassie (*pointedly*) Me too, Marie. I'm sure I've seen her.
Deirdre No.
Marie Just outside the house there.
Deirdre Wasn't me.
Marie So you got caught in the rain?

Deirdre gives no response

You shouldn't be out without a coat in this weather; you'll catch your death.

Deirdre shrugs

Will your mother be worrying about you?

Deirdre shakes her head

Nora The woman next door's got a phone love; you could pop in there and give her a ring, sure she'll be worrying about you with everything going on.
Deirdre She's out.
Nora (*distracted by the TV*) Oh look at that one, oh he's the kind that'll sing, I love it when they do that.

There is a pause

Marie I'll need to get my dinner if we are going out tonight. You'll take something Cassie?
Cassie No, no, I told you.
Marie Nora?
Nora (*with her eyes on the screen*) No you're all right pet, we've a fry to eat when Danny gets in . . . (*At the TV*) Oh here he goes, look Cassie! (*Singing along*) "You are the sunshine of my life . . ." Oh do you see him Cassie!?
Cassie I hate when they do that, it's just embarrassing.

Marie fetches herself a plate of food. She divides half its contents onto another plate which she gives to Deirdre

Deirdre takes the plate without comment

There is another shot, more distant

Marie, Cassie and Nora look at each other, Deirdre keeps her eyes on the screen

Marie Turn the sound up on that will you, Nora?

Nora turns the sound up

Nora (*to Deirdre*) Did you see what's going on out there?

Deirdre shakes her head

You didn't see nothing?

Deirdre (*with her mouth full and eyes on the screen*) Buses burning and Brits everywhere.

Nora (*to the others*) Wonder what it's all about?

Cassie shakes her head. Marie looks at her watch

When's the next news, Marie?

Marie Six thirty.

Nora (*turning back to the TV*) Oh look! Oh will you look!

Marie What?

Nora They've got a weekend in the Caribbean! Oh look, Cassie!

Cassie I see it.

Nora Oh wouldn't that be great! She looks pleased, doesn't she?

Cassie I suppose she's got a weekend to find something better than the singing spring onion she picked for herself there.

Nora Oh I think he's lovely. What do you think, Marie?

Marie (*not listening*) Hmmm?

Cassie (*turning back to Deirdre*) That's quite a walk from the school down to here.

No response from Deirdre

You've got friends down here then?

There is still no response from Deirdre

Maybe that's where I've seen you, visiting your friends round here.

Deirdre (*to Marie*) Can I get another cup of tea, please?

Marie (*surprised*) Yes of course.

Cassie Yes it's the best café in the road here.

Marie throws Cassie a look and goes to pour another cup

Nora Have you nothing warmer to wear pet, sure you'll be catching a chill there.

Deirdre (*quietly*) I'm OK.

Nora What's that?

Deirdre I'm OK!

Nora I think I'm going deaf, Cassie.

Cassie No I don't think you are, Mummy. (*To Deirdre*) No, I just thought I saw you outside there, just about a quarter of an hour ago, at the end of the path.

Marie (*struck*) Did you see her?

Cassie I'd swear I did.

Deirdre (*muttering*) No.

Cassie What?
Deirdre It wasn't me.
Cassie Must've been some other wee girl in a white dress then.

Nora flaps a hand at Cassie trying to get her attention. She mouths the word "glue"

What, Mummy?
Nora (*flustered*) Nothing, I was just looking at these three girls here—oh it's the adverts . . . (*She mouths again "glue"*)

Deirdre is apparently watching the screen, oblivious

Cassie What?
Nora (*with a piercing whisper*) Glue!

Deirdre does not react

Cassie looks at her speculatively

Cassie Hmmm . . . maybe.

Marie hands Deirdre another cup of tea; she exchanges another look with Cassie

Deirdre I've seen you though.
Nora Who pet?
Deirdre (*looking at Cassie*) Her.
Cassie Have you though? Where was that?
Deirdre It was a long time ago, years ago.
Nora You couldn't miss her anyway.
Cassie (*to Deirdre*) What are you talking about?

Deirdre gives no response

Well where, then?

Deirdre shrugs

It's the Night of the Living Dead here, Marie . . . So you know who I am? You know my name?

Deirdre gives no response

I'm Cassie Ryan and this is my mother Nora and this is Marie Donnelly.

Deirdre gives a brief nod

So what's your name?
Deirdre (*muttering*) Deirdre.
Cassie What?
Deirdre Deirdre.
Cassie Deirdre what?

Deirdre gives no response

Deirdre what?

Deirdre (*to Marie*) Can I use your bathroom, please?
Marie Sure you can love; it's first left in the hall there.

Deirdre exits

Nora has become absorbed in the TV again. Cassie and Marie look at each other

Cassie (*quietly*) Is that her?
Marie It is.
Cassie I saw her as well.
Marie Did you?
Cassie End of the path there. Staring.
Nora (*with her eyes on the screen*) What did she say her second name was?
Cassie (*louder*) She didn't, Mummy.
Nora Deirdre—there was a Deirdre McMahon used to live up there—sure but she'd be twenty-five now at least . . .
Cassie Is it time for the news yet?
Marie Oh here, put it on. (*She switches off the TV*)

Cassie moves to the radio

The Lights change

Deirdre I need a knife. A wee blade of my own. It's quieter than a gun. You can hold it quiet in your hand. Maybe I'd like that. (*Pause*) I see a lot of things. This time I saw a man holding another man outside the circle of light the street lamp made on the road. He kept him pinned to the wall in the dark with a wee blade. It was the neatest thing you ever saw, wee and thin, like he had a metal finger he could point where he liked and he was saying, "Is that the truth then? Is that the truth?" but the other man never says anything back at all and I thought to myself that maybe it wasn't a question, maybe it was the knife he was talking about. It was the truth. I thought I'd like that. A wee bit of hard truth you could hold in your hand and point where you liked.

The Lights change

Nora Well, if that wasn't a pack of lies what was it?
Cassie You'd think if they didn't know what was going on they'd just tell you 'stead of making it up for themselves.
Marie I hate it when that's all they give you, "reports of casualties" and you're left wondering who or how many.
Cassie Sounds like they've got someone though, doesn't it?

Marie moves over to put the TV back on

Nora Have you got your pass for tomorrow?
Marie I did, but they've put the wrong date on it.
Nora Sure they'll not bother about it, they're nice as anything at the Kesh these days.
Marie It's some change isn't it?

Nora Something to be grateful for Marie, we've a lot to weigh us down, the two of us; one man dead and the other in a prison cell. A lot to weep over.

Cassie And here's me never stopped dancing since they took mine away.

Nora Cassie!

Cassie Sure they did me a favour when they lifted him.

Marie (*laughing*) You'll be telling me next you made the phone call.

Nora Marie!

Cassie I did not, a useless bastard he may be, but he doesn't deserve what he's had in there, no one does.

Nora Oh do you remember the night they took Joe? You should've seen me, Marie.

Cassie She was something that night, Andytown's own Incredible Hulk, "Don't get me angry"!

Nora Well Marie, there was wee Cassie——

Cassie Wee? I'm wee again am I?

Nora —just a week out the hospital with the stitches still in from the section that gave us Teresa, and I open my door and here she is running up the road——

Cassie That was when we had our own house, you know, at the end there——

Nora Squealing "Mummy! Mummy!"——

Cassie —one hand clutching my stomach 'cause I'm sure the whole lot's going to fall out.

Nora —"Mummy! Mummy! They're taking Joe!" Well I just felt my blood rise——

Cassie She was a lioness. She was.

Nora —I marched back up the road and here they were, dragging the poor man out of his own house without even a pair of shoes on his feet——

Cassie He'd been snoring away in front of the football, toasting his toes, with a pie in one hand and a can in the other.

Nora Sure he'd not been ready for any trouble; why would he be?

Cassie And the rest of them are throwing everything every which way and all over the house and the baby's screaming and the child's calling for her daddy——

Nora And he keeps his hand tight round this pie the whole time they were dragging him away. And I goes up to this big R.U.C. man and I says——

Cassie She picked the biggest.

Nora I says, "What's the charges? Where's your warrants?"

Cassie And he's peering down at her like he's a mountain and she's a beetle at the bottom of it.

Nora And he says "And who are you?" And I says, "I'm that boy's mother-in-law, and before you take him you'll have to answer to me!"

Cassie Can you beat it, Marie?

Nora And he says, "You get out of our way Mrs or it'll be the worse for you."

Cassie He didn't say it as nice as that Mummy, there was a few fucking old . . .

Nora *We* do not need to use language like that Cassie! "Out the way or it'll be the worse for you," he says. Oh he was a big bastard Marie. "Oh," I says, "Oh would you strike a woman that could be your own mother? Would you now?" (*She starts to laugh*)

Marie What happened?

Cassie Wallop! Knocked her straight through the hedge.

Nora (*still laughing*) Would you hit a mother? Sure I got my answer on the end of his fist.

Cassie Nearly choked on her false teeth.

Nora I did.

Cassie I didn't know which of them to go to first, Joe, or Mummy in the hedge with her little legs waving in the air.

Nora (*wiping her eyes, still laughing*) Oh—oh but that was a terrible night. (*Getting serious*) Sure, when they took our Martin there was no one for me to battle with. He just never came home, his dinner drying up and waiting and waiting till you knew something had happened ... then waiting some more.

Marie It was the same with our Davey.

Nora And him only a child. The pain of that just killed your mummy, didn't it Marie? ... Just finished her off.

There is a pause

I wish our Danny would get safe home.

Cassie Well I'm telling you Marie. It's Mummy here had the temper in our house. We were all terrified to leave our shoelaces undone.

Nora Your daddy had a temper!

Cassie Daddy! I'll tell you how much he could stand up for himself. He hated eggs.

Marie So?

Cassie So a big yellow-eyed egg he got in the middle of his fry every Saturday and never said a word about it.

Nora (*getting sharp*) He had a temper when he had a drink in him.

Cassie (*sharp back*) If he was pushed.

Nora He had a temper.

Cassie My daddy never had a word to say for himself.

Marie I wonder what that wee girl's doing in the bathroom all this time?

All look towards the door

Marie (*getting up, listening*) She's taking a shower.

Nora She's not!

Marie I can hear her.

Cassie Well do you like the cheek of that?

Marie I better put the hot water on, she'll have the tank emptied.

Cassie Marie!

Nora She looked like she could do with a wash.

Cassie (*getting up*) I'm going to bang on that door.

Marie Oh leave her, Cassie.

Cassie Leave her!?

Nora That child needs help from someone.

Cassie She needs something Mummy, or she's after something. I wonder you can have her in the house, Marie.

Marie Well—maybe we'll find out what's been going on.

Cassie You'd be better asking questions of a can of beans than that one.

Marie Is the road block still there?

Cassie crosses to the window to look

Cassie There's still a crowd of them up the top there.

Marie I was wanting out with my crumbs.

Nora Crumbs?

Marie For the birds.

Nora What do you want to do that for?

Marie I just like to.

Nora I thought birds were one thing that could look out for themselves in this town.

Marie It's only crusts; I just like to feed them.

Cassie You remember when Marie was a child, Mummy, and they'd been burnt out, had to spend a few months in those big flats.

Marie That's when I got started, I'd throw crusts out the window and see if the birds could get them before they hit the ground. And they did you know, they never let a scrap go to waste.

Cassie (*sarcastically*) Amazing isn't it Mummy?

Marie I like the birds.

Deirdre enters the room, hair wet, wrapped in a towel

All turn and gape at her

Deirdre Do you have a hair-dryer?

There is a pause

Marie It's in the bedroom.

Deirdre exits

Cassie (*calling after her*) Just make yourself at home!

Nora She'd nothing on at all!

Cassie We saw.

Nora That wee girl is trouble, Marie.

Cassie You tell her, Mummy.

Marie Well you wouldn't have me turn her out on the street in a towel would you?

There is a pause

Cassie looks out the window again

Cassie Oh I think they're moving off. They'll be around the place for the rest of the night, but. . . .

Marie Still, maybe we'll get out to the club after all.

Nora Oh you're coming, Marie? Oh that's great.

Marie Sure I've nothing to keep me in now, have I?

Cassie (*meaningfully*) Not as long as you get her clear of the house before you go.

Marie (*moving to the door*) I'll see if I can get Brendan to go down now.

Cassie Is he sleeping better?

Marie Well he goes down all right; then he's up in the night.

Cassie (*to Nora*) Bad dreams.

Marie He thinks he sees his daddy.

Nora Sure, but he was only a baby.

Marie One of the wee boys at the school has been tormenting him, saying his daddy had his head blown off.

Nora Oh that's cruel! That's cruel!

Marie So he's dreaming about it.

Nora Wee boys are terrible cruel.

Cassie Tell her what you say to him, Marie.

Marie I just bring him into the fire and I hold him and I rock him and I say—(*getting dreamy*) Your daddy was a good man and a brave man and he did the best he could and he's in heaven watching out for you and when you're good he's happy, he's smiling at you and that's what keeps us all together, keeps me going, keeps me strong because I know your daddy can see us . . .

There is a pause

Nora (*choked*) Marie—that's lovely. (*She gulps*) I'll away and get Danny's fry on, Cassie.

Nora exits hurriedly

Marie (*looking at Cassie*) I know Cassie, but he's a child; it's good for him to hear it like that.

Cassie does not respond

I know, I know he was no saint—but I miss him.

Cassie I know you do.

There is a pause

(*With a sudden vehemence*) Oh Marie, I wish I was out of this place!

Marie Cassie?

Cassie I'll see you later, better go and find what the kids have left of my sacred wee brother's dinner.

Cassie leaves the acting area

Lighting change

Oh my daddy was a lovely man. Gentle. He'd hold you in his lap like you had fur and he didn't want to ruffle it. He held me like that anyway. There's been men that've told me I'm pretty and men that've told me I'm clever and men that've sworn I'm some kind of angel come down to pull them out of a sea of whisky and give them the kiss of life. (*Pause*) Lying hounds every one of them. (*Pause*) My daddy said I was the best girl that ever stirred her daddy's tea for him. The best girl that ever sat on his lap or combed his hair or did any of the wee things he wasn't fit to do for himself. My daddy said I was special. (*Pause*) My daddy never lied to me. So it must have been me that lied to him.

Cassie exits

Lights revert to normal

Marie is slowly tidying up and shredding bread for the birds

Marie I like the pigeons. I saw a pigeon fly across the sky and when it crossed the clouds it was black but when it flew past the roofs it was white. It could fly as far as it liked but it never went further than Turf Lodge from what I could see. (*Pause*) I used to watch for that bird, the only white bird that wasn't a seagull. (*Pause*) He wasn't even the man they wanted, but they shot him; that made him the man they wanted. (*Pause*) You have to imagine the four of them. All men you'd look at twice one way or another. Michael, my husband, because he had that strong feel to him. You felt it in the back of your neck when he came in a room. People turned to look without knowing why. Davey, my brother now, you'd look again but you'd say, what's that wee boy doing in his daddy's jacket. Nineteen and he looks more like nine, though they've put age in his eyes for him now. He's got old eyes now. Martin, Cassie's brother, you'd look and you'd cross the street in case he caught your eye and decided he didn't like the look of *you*, he's got the kind of eyebrows that chop short conversations, slamming a glower on his face like two fists hitting a table—and Joe, Cassie's husband. You'd look at him to see what the joke was, Joe's always laughing, Joe's always where the crack is. (*Pause*) Davey's in the Kesh. Martin's in the Kesh. Joe's in the Kesh—and Michael is dead. (*Pause*) They didn't really go round together, the four of them, just every odd Saturday they'd be in here playing cards till they were three of them broke and Joe stuffed with beer and winnings. Singing till they were too drunk to remember the words then waking and eating and drinking some more till they were drunk enough to make up their own. Sure it was a party they had. And Davey felt like a man and Martin smiled and Joe sang almost in tune and Michael would tell me he loved me over and over till he'd made a song out of that. (*Pause*) Sometimes he said he loved me when he'd no drink in him at all. Sometimes he even did that.

Marie finishes tidying and exits

Deirdre enters the empty room. She has her hair swept back, her face made up. She is wearing tight white jeans and a shiny white top. She has jewellery on. She looks stunning. She also looks about twenty-one. She stands for a moment, admiring herself then wanders over to look at the portrait of Michael. She studies it, then almost leisurely reaches behind it and removes the money Cassie has hidden there

Deirdre exits

Black-out

Scene 2

The Club

This could be a community hall or even an ancient warehouse but it has been jazzed up with glitterballs and spots. The chairs and tables are cheap and battered. There are double doors at the back of the room. Marie, Nora and Cassie have got themselves a table overlooking the small dance floor. There is a small stand, like a lectern, on one side of it. The place is crowded, bright with the colours of the women's dresses and great misty clouds of cigarette smoke whorling in the fans. Cassie's dress is quite revealing though not extravagantly so. It is silent. The three women are standing by their chairs, heads bowed as if by a grave-side. No one moves, they speak in whispers

Marie I didn't know him.

Cassie There's that cramp again, in my leg, I'll wobble.

Nora That's his aunty there, is it not? She shouldn't be here drinking sure she shouldn't.

Marie Can't put a face to him at all.

Cassie My *shoes*, a size too small and I've swelled with the heat. Oh God, don't let me fall off them.

Nora His mother's sister-in-law's sister; it's close enough. She should be with that poor woman.

Marie Was he young?

Cassie Just a boy too.

Nora Is that not a minute over?

Marie Is that not a minute now?

Cassie Can I get off my feet?

There is a sudden burst of music and a loud buzz of talk. The women shout over this as they claim their seats with jackets and handbags

Marie Did you get my ticket for the competition, Cassie?

Cassie I got us all ten.

Nora Ten?

Marie Money to burn.

Cassie I'm feeling lucky.

Marie So it's a gin and lime and a black Russian for you, Nora?

Nora No, I'll get these.

Cassie Sure I'll get them.

Marie (*waving a fiver at the waitress*) No you're all right, I've my money in my hand.

Cassie Let's have a kitty then, fiver in and start us with doubles, Marie.

Marie I can't catch her eye.

Nora Did you know him then, the poor wee boy?

Cassie It was him with the dog.

Nora At the chemist's?

Cassie His brother.

Marie Always seems such a long minute.

Nora I was just in that chemist's today.

Marie I hate it. Never know what to fill my head with.

Nora They still hadn't got my prescription in.

Marie I didn't know him. What can you fill your head with if you can't picture his face?

Cassie You'd know him if you saw him. Just nineteen, trying to grow a moustache like dust on a ledge.

Nora His mother's youngest. The last one at home.

Marie (*shivering*) I still can't see him. I just think of coffins.

Nora She's all on her own now. All on her own.

Cassie Marie, will you hurry up getting that drink, it's the only nourishment I've got coming to me today. This is going to be the wildest of wild nights. I'm telling you, Mummy, all the times I've been coming here, the best ones have always been when we've come on our own, just the three of us.

Marie waves her money for the waitress again

Marie exits

Nora Remember the first we knew of what happened to Michael was when they asked us to stand for him?

Cassie Marie had never been out of her house, never told a soul till we came in to her.

Nora Oh, but he was well respected.

Cassie Just sitting by the fire and the fire dead for hours and the baby crying and crying . . .

Nora They sang for him as well, do you remember?

Cassie Her just sitting there.

Nora He's still missed; there's some men you don't forget.

Cassie He was popular, I'll say that for him.

Nora He was.

Marie returns with two glasses for each of them balanced on a tray

Nora Oh Marie, do you remember when my Sean took all that money off your Michael?

Marie (*smiling*) Betting on a dog that never was.

Nora turns to relate the story to Cassie who doesn't display much interest, she's heard it before

Nora He had some terrible tall stories, your daddy.

Marie He says, "I know a dog can run up the side of a wall." If he'd left it at a ten pound bet we'd've been all right . . .

Nora Oh Sean could be bold.

Marie I can hear him yet. "Now Michael," he says, "I wouldn't want to take your money."

Nora Egging him on . . .

Marie Did I tell you the plotting and planning that was spent on that idea? Grown men, sitting in our front room with cans and sandwiches and paper and pens and rulers, little scale drawings of walls, talk of alsatians and dobermans and greyhounds and wind speed and how if Sean was talking about a terrier then he was a liar for sure. They took it so seriously.

Nora Well it was a two hundred pound bet by then. It was serious.

Marie The drinking was serious. There'd been some serious drinking when they all went out the back of the club and saw a little terrier dog jump a ten foot wall.

Nora (*shaking her head*) Two hundred pounds.

Marie It was worse Nora. That car we gave you was worth at least five hundred with its wheels on.

Nora I don't know where they found that cat.

Marie I don't know who cut the tail off it but they should be ashamed of themselves.

Nora And dressing it in my good mohair jumper. I never saw that jumper again.

Marie Well you wouldn't, the jumper and the cat were half way to Galway before anyone had even a quarter sobered up and looking no more like a terrier than they ever could unless you were looking through the bottom of a whisky glass. And when Michael found out he just laughed. The man's sense of humour nearly ruined us. Laughed himself black in the face and started plotting how to get that car back off your Sean.

Nora We'd sold it by then.

Marie He had all these schemes—(*quieter*) never got to try them though.

Nora (*matching Marie's tone*) And Sean dead himself just three months after . . .

There is a pause

Cassie Are we going to drink to that, then?

Marie What?

Cassie The dear departed?

Nora Cassie!

Cassie Well, are we going to drink to something?

Marie laughs

Marie Come on then.

Marie clinks her glass with Cassie's

Cassie (*raising her glass*) To the bold girls.

Nora And who are they?

Cassie That's us.

Nora There's only one bold girl here, Cassie Ryan, and she's broadcasting it to the world.

Cassie What do you mean?
Nora What do you think I mean?
Cassie Well I don't know, Mummy, that's why I'm asking.
Nora And you with your man inside.
Cassie And what about him?
Nora What about you?
Marie Oh look do you see B.T. and that other boy looking over here?
What's on their mind do you think?
Nora Oh, we're great entertainment tonight, Marie.
Cassie Mummy if there's something on your mind, would you just out and
say it please?
Marie (*looking out past the dance floor*) Oh here's Jimmy going to call out
the numbers. Have you got your tickets, girls?

Cassie is still confronting a stony-faced Nora

Cassie Come on!
Marie Cassie, you've got them all in your bag there.
Cassie All what?
Marie Come on down, he's calling out the numbers.
Cassie Oh—right. (*She rummages in her bag*)
Marie Come on, he's called one already.
Nora What was that one Marie? I didn't hear him right.
Marie Ninety-six.
Nora Have we got a ninety-six Cassie?
Cassie (*spreading the tickets to look; sullenly*) No.
Marie And—seventy-two.
Nora Seventy-two Cassie?
Cassie No.
Marie Eh—wait a minute ... Oh he's dropped the cards Nora!
Nora Jimmy Dooley was on the whisky before he was weaned.
Marie Here we are—one hundred and three.
Cassie (*picking out a card*) One hundred and three, that's your ticket Marie.
Marie What?
Cassie One hundred and three. Look.
Marie That's not mine!
Cassie It is so, I got you the first ten.
Nora Go on Marie, they're waiting on you!
Marie Oh no Nora, you take it!
Cassie Go *on*, Marie!
Marie Oh I hate standing out in front of everyone. (*She moves to cross to the
dance floor and looks back*) You'll shout the prices out to me?
Cassie Yes! Go *on*!

*Marie goes to stand behind the lectern on the dance floor, smiling round her
nervously*

Cassie and Nora take a long swig of their drinks. The don't look at each other

Nora Oh she's shaking. Look, we'll need to keep her right, Cassie.

Cassie So is it because I've no bra on, is that what's eating you?
Nora (*shocked*) You've no bra on!
Cassie Well, where did you think I would fit it under this?
Nora Cassie Ryan, you're sitting here, bare-breasted in front of the whole town!
Cassie Well, you didn't notice did you?
Nora I noticed that dress!
Cassie Good.
Nora There's nothing good about it.
Cassie What's that? (*Peering*) A Black and Decker drill? Ninety-five pounds, what do you say?
Nora No—fifty-nine pounds, ninety-nine.
Cassie Could be right.

Marie looks up at Cassie and Nora anxiously

Cassie (*shouting across to Marie*) Fifty-nine, ninety-nine.

Nora shows five, and three nines with her fingers

Marie nods and starts writing on a big sheet of paper in front of her

Joe always liked this dress.
Nora Joe isn't here, is he?
Cassie Oh so I should just get back in my box and wear bin liners till he's out should I?
Nora You know there's been talk.
Cassie I don't know, what talk?

Marie displays her price

Nora Did she get it?

Cassie looks at Marie

Marie crumples the piece of paper

Cassie No ... What talk?

Marie prepares a fresh sheet of paper

Nora (*peering*) What's this coming now?
Cassie A tea set. What talk, Mummy?
Nora Danny said one of the boys had words with him.

Cassie says nothing. She takes a long drink

That'd be thirty pounds or so, what do you think?

Cassie still says nothing

Nora mimes thirty at Marie

Marie nods and writes

So Danny says to me, "Mummy, I know our Cassie isn't doing a line and so do you, but there's plenty will think she is."

Cassie And what business is it of Danny's?

Nora He's looking out for you, Cassie.

Cassie And what business is it of the boys?

Nora I should think they're thinking of Joe.

Cassie They might've thought of him before they let him take the rap for a job he wouldn't have had the brains to understand if they'd tattooed it on his wrist.

Nora You're just determined to let the world think the worst of you, are you?

Cassie I don't care what the world thinks. (*Peering*) Computer games. Eighteen pounds, ninety-five.

Nora Twenty-five pounds.

Cassie Eighteen ninety-five, I've seen them in a catalogue. (*Shouting*) Eighteen ninety-five. (*She mimes the numbers*)

Marie writes

Nora You're bringing shame on this family, Cassie.

Cassie Well I won't be the first.

Nora What do you mean?

Cassie Our Martin was never too good at keeping his belt buckle fastened, was he?

Nora Your brother was a good boy, the best boy a mother ever——

Cassie (*interrupting*) Well, you tell that to the wee girl in Turf Lodge.

Marie crumples another sheet of paper

   Oh she just missed it!

Nora That was not Martin's child.

Cassie Oh it just borrowed that nose and that red hair off another friend of the family did it? (*Peering*) A magi-mix, oh it'd be great if she got that.

Nora I asked her to her face, I said, if you can look me in the eye and swear by the Virgin that this is my grandchild I'll not see you short, just look me in the eye and tell me.

Cassie Forty-five pounds! Marie! (*She mimes*) Forty-five pounds!

Nora And all she said was, I'm not wanting your money, Mrs Ryan.

Cassie Do you know you never put a plate of food in front of me before he had his.

Nora She was nothing be a wee hoor.

Marie holds up her sheet

Cassie Oh she's put eighty-nine ninety-nine. Oh Marie!

Nora What has food got to do with it?

Cassie The only time you gave me food before him was when I was to serve him. I never *once* got my dinner before he'd his in his mouth. Not *once*.

Nora What are you talking about Cassie?

Marie I've got it! (*She waves at Nora and Cassie excitedly*)

Cassie Oh Mummy! She's won the magi-mix!

Marie stands with her hands up in triumph then stares as:

Deirdre walks over the dance floor to Marie carrying her prize

There is ragged applause

Deirdre hands the big box over with a model's grin

Marie Thanks.

Deirdre turns and smiles at the applause

Marie wanders to the side of the dance floor where Nora and Cassie are waiting for her

Cassie Was that your white top, Marie?

Marie It looked like it. It looked like my earrings as well.

Nora Did you not used to have a pair of white trousers like that, Marie?

Marie I did. They were exactly like that.

Nora That wee girl is trouble.

Cassie (*moving towards her*) And I'm going to find out what kind.

Marie Cassie, wait.

Marie catches Cassie's arm

She's not going anywhere.

Cassie Marie, when will you stand up for yourself? You're a mug! That girl's making a fool of you!

Marie And when I get the chance I'll hear what she has to say but it won't be here with half the town hearing it as well Cassie!

Cassie hesitates

Nora Well I'm dry, I think we should get ourselves another drink.

Marie That's a great idea, Nora. What'll you have?

Nora No, no, we'll use the kitty, like before.

Cassie I'll get them.

Marie No, I'll do it, Cassie.

Cassie *I'll get them.*

Marie and Nora sit down

Lighting change

Cassie (*moving to the bar*) My Mummy taught me how to raise my family. How to love them, how to spoil them. Spoil the wee girls with housework and reproaches, the length of their skirts and the colour of their lips: how they sit, how they slouch, how they don't give their fathers peace, how they talk, how they talk back, how they'll come to no good if they carry on like that. They're bold and bad and broken at fourteen but you love them as you love yourself . . . that's why you hurt them so much. (*Pause*) Ruin the boys, tell them they're noisy and big and bold and their boots are too muddy, "Clear that mess up for me Cassie." Tell them to leave their fathers in peace and come to their mummy for a cuddle, tell them they'll always be your own wee man, always your own bold wee man and you love them better than you love their daddy, you love them best of all—that's why they hurt you so much.

Lights revert to previous level

Dance music plays behind the talk

Cassie picks up a tray with another double round on it and moves back to the table

Nora (*in the middle of telling a story*) That's your woman up the street came to me crying and sobbing: her man lifted, her kids running wild, the phone and the electric off and on again as often as she could drag herself up the town to argue with them. "Oh Nora," she says, "Nora I don't know what to do." I says "Well Sheila, for a start you could wash those front windows of yours and when you've done that you better do the curtains as well for the whole street will be able to see the colour of them then." "Oh Nora," she says, "I'm living in hell, I'm just living in hell." "Well," I says, "If this is hell it could do with a lick of paint and I've a couple of tins left over from my bedroom I could lend you." Oh but she never stirred herself to get it done. Her kids are just wild wee hoods, took that paint and painted her lawn roseblush white, took the magnolia and went out painting F—(*She nods "you know the word I mean"*) the I.R.A. on all the walls, but you could hardly read it. That's the beauty of that magnolia, it'll blend in with just anything. (*She takes a drink*)

Marie (*drinking*) Thanks, Cassie. You did a lovely job in your bedroom with that magnolia, Nora.

Nora It was nice, it was, while it lasted.

Cassie That was the damp brought it all down.

Marie No!

Cassie Oh, the paper's hanging off the wall in there.

Nora Still I'll get my front room nice again.

Marie It'll look great with that material you showed me, sure it will.

Nora Oh but I'll never have my bamboo suite again. Do you remember my bamboo suite, Marie?

Marie It was lovely.

Cassie Are you coming up dancing Marie?

Marie Oh but there's no one else up yet.

Cassie So?

Nora And I had those big potted ferns, remember, just like I saw it in the magazine.

Cassie Mummy, come dancing with me.

Nora I'm not dancing, Cassie, what do you think this is, a wedding? Oh Marie, it just sickened the heart out of me when that suite got broke.

Cassie Oh your man's still watching us. I think he's got his eye on you Mummy. (*She starts dancing in her chair to the music*)

Nora Sit at peace, Cassie. Now your wee boy, he went round it didn't he? Comes in my door like he's Ireland's best chance at the Olympics, right through the room and he says, "Sorry Mrs," he does, nice soft wee voice and him running for his life. But he runs *round* my lovely bamboo suite and jumps out the window.

Cassie starts to sing along with the music

And then the Brits are through and do they not run over it? Boots like anvils, they were wearing my suite before I'd time to open my mouth. And then kicking and swearing and trying to pull their feet out of it.

Cassie Marie knows, Mummy, you told her half an hour after it happened and you've never stopped telling her.

Nora Cassie stop wriggling about.

Cassie I'm just giving your man there something to look at.

Nora 'Course I tried to stop them . . .

Marie Oh your poor ribs.

Nora Well I thought this one looked like he'd a bit of sense, Marie.

Cassie snorts

Well he was older than the rest, you know, they're just young animals but he looked like Michael Aspel.

Cassie Do you not love this song Marie?

Nora So I says, "You'll not wreck my house, son," 'course he keeps coming so I says——

Cassie ⎱
Nora ⎰ *(together, mimicking Nora's tone)* "Oh but you'll not hit a woman."

Marie That was an awful dig he gave you.

Nora I'd those ribs taped for months. Oh but my bamboo suite, Marie. Two hundred pounds and I'd only had it a week. I'd saved, ten months it took me, sliding a note out of Sean's pocket every time he was too puddled to know how many fivers he'd poured down his throat.

Cassie Poor daddy.

Nora Easy to see you didn't have the carpet to mop up after him.

Cassie Well I'm up for a dance myself.

Cassie gets up and crosses to the dance floor and starts to dance. Marie and Nora gape at her

Nora Holy Mother of God, what is she doing!?

Marie I don't know, Nora.

Nora Oh Marie get up with her!

Marie What!

Nora We can't leave her on her own there, performing for the whole town!

Cassie's dancing becomes more extravagant

Nora Marie!

Marie *(getting up)* Oh Nora I don't even like dancing.

Marie crosses over and joins Cassie who beams, applauding her. Marie starts shuffling cautiously from foot to foot

Cassie I'm telling you this is a great diet Marie, you really feel the benefit of the gin.

Marie Well maybe you should go easy now, Cassie.

Cassie Oh I'm a long way from lockjawed.

Nora is beckoning at them frantically

Marie Your mummy's asking us to come and sit down.
Cassie The song's just started.

Marie glances round nervously

What? Are they all watching us?
Marie They are.
Cassie Let them.
Marie (*with a shaky laugh*) Feel a bit like the last meat pie in the shop out here, Cassie.
Cassie Well let them stay hungry. They can just look and think what they like.
Marie Cassie, what's wrong?
Cassie Oh I'm just bad Marie, didn't you know?
Marie No. I never knew that.
Cassie You remember that wee girl in Turf Lodge, the one Martin couldn't get enough of? She was a decent wee girl. She's bad now. Ask my mummy.
Marie Have you had words?
Cassie He's out in less than a year, Marie.
Marie *Martin*!?
Cassie Joe.
Marie I know. It'll be all right Cassie.

They stop dancing, they look at each other

It'll be all right, Cassie.
Cassie I tell you Marie I can't stand the smell of him. The greasy, grinning, beer bellied *smell* of him. And he's winking away about all he's been dreaming of, wriggling his fat fingers over me like I'm a poke of chips—I don't want him in the house in my *bed,* Marie.
Marie You'll cope.
Cassie Oh I'm just bad. I am.
Marie Don't. Don't say that about yourself.
Cassie I'll go crazy.
Marie I won't let you. You won't get a chance Cassie, I'll just be across the road, I won't let you go crazy. You just see what you'll get if you try it.

Slowly Cassie smiles at her

(*Putting a hand on Cassie's arm*) Now will you come and sit down?

The doors at the back bang open

Hard white light floods everything

Oh Jesus it's a raid!

All the women freeze, legs apart, arms raised as if they're being searched

The same hard light stays on them

Deirdre Brick in your hand, hard in your hand, hit skin and it'll burst open and bleed, hit bones and they'll break, you can hear them break, hear them snap.

Marie Why are you asking my name, you know my name.

Deirdre Smell the petrol, lungs full of the smell of it. Blow it out again and you'll be breathing fire. Throw fire in a bottle and it runs everywhere like it's water.

Marie Everyone knows where I live.

Deirdre Get a car, fast car, drive it till its wheels burn, leave it smoking, burning, exploding.

Marie Everyone knows all about me, don't they? So what do you want to know? What do you want?

Deirdre The whole town's a prison, smash chunks off the walls 'cause we're all in a prison.

Cut the hard white light

Cassie (*running up to the table*) Mummy are you all right?

Nora I'm fine, I was just thinking about getting another drink here.

Cassie I was sure you would hit someone again.

Nora I won't say I didn't think about it. They searched me Cassie!

Cassie I saw. I thought you'd give her a swipe in the gub.

Nora Terrible cold hands she had.

Cassie Here where's my drink?

Nora I gave it to that big peeler there.

Cassie What? What did you do that for?

Nora Well he was leaning on that table over there just shouting in Bobby's face and I'm looking down and here's his socks.

Marie Where?

Nora On his feet, in his boots. Pale blue socks, you could see the whole back of his heel there, I don't think his boots were fitting too well. So your drink was just on the edge here Cassie, (*She demonstrates with an empty glass*) so I just gave it a wee nudge. (*She knocks it over*) Poured in as neat as you please. Oh he was desperate angry. I just stared him down.

Cassie (*starting to laugh*) Oh you're doing your bit for the struggle all right, Mummy.

Marie Give them all wet socks!

Nora Here, I'll get you another one Cassie. (*She waves for a waitress*)

Cassie Should've known they'd be in tonight.

Marie They're saying it was a break-out from the Crumlin Road.

Cassie Is that what was happening?

Marie That's what I heard up at the bar there. Maybe three of them got away.

Cassie Oh it'll be road blocks the rest of the night then.

Nora (*calling*) Can we get a drink here?

Deirdre comes up to their table with a tray

Marie, Nora and Cassie stare at her

Deirdre What're you having?

There is a pause

Marie Well, the jeans don't fit any more so they're yours and welcome and I
never was desperate fond of that top so you can have it, but those earrings
were a present from my husband so I'll be having them back.

*Deirdre fingers the earrings for a minute then unfastens them and hands them
over*

Marie Thank you. Now it's a Black Russian, a gin and lime and a Pernod
and blackcurrant.

Deirdre nods, and turns on her heel

Cassie Well! Marie!
Marie What?
Cassie I see Oxfam's come to Andersonstown. Any time we want a new
outfit we'll know where to come!
Marie Would you've had her strip where she stood?
Cassie I'd've had an explanation out of her!
Marie She was probably wanting new clothes.
Cassie And wasn't she lucky that Mother Teresa was ready to hand them
over!
Nora You should've said something to her, Marie.

Marie just shakes her head

Cassie You're not letting her away with it altogether?
Marie She's a look about her.

Nora and Cassie look at each other

Nora What do you mean?
Marie I don't know. I don't know what it's got me thinking of but she's a
look about her.
Cassie She's not a ghost Marie.
Nora She's a thieving wee hood.
Marie It's like she's looking for something.
Cassie Trouble.

Marie just shakes her head again

Nora I don't know, Marie. (*Lighting up a cigarette*) Cassie's right, she's
making a mug out of you. Oh, will you look at that. (*She shows them her
hand which is trembling violently*)
Cassie It's the D.T.'s.
Nora It's the R.U.C.
Cassie Oh don't let it get to you.
Nora So let's see your hand!

Cassie holds hers out, it is also shaking

Cassie It's our life style Mummy, we'll have to change our life style.
Nora Is that right?
Cassie We're living too fast so we are, it's the same problem the film stars
have, we'll burn ourselves out with all the excitement.

Nora Me and Joan Collins both.
Cassie You can write articles for the women's magazines, "Stop and Search, would your manicure stand up to the *closest* inspection?"
Nora Let's see Marie's hand there.

Marie is lost in her own thoughts

Cassie pulls Marie's hand out, Nora and Cassie study it

Cassie Steady as a rock.
Nora Ah she's got a clear conscience.
Cassie Either that or she's in a coma, are you with us, Marie?
Marie Hmmm?
Nora Wired up but not plugged in.
Marie Are you reading my palm?
Cassie I will if you like.

Deirdre approaches their table with a tray of drinks

Cassie glances up at her, then bends theatrically over Marie's hand

Cassie Oh, you're going to meet a dark stranger Marie, all in white but with a black wee heart. You better watch out for she'll thieve the clothes off your back but you'll not have peace till you nail the wee snake down and ask her what she's up to.
Deirdre (*handing out the drinks correctly*) Black Russian—gin and lime— Pernod and blackcurrant.
Cassie So what about you Deirdre, if it is Deirdre?
Deirdre It is.
Marie Cassie . . .
Cassie I hope you've not taken a fancy to anything else that's caught your eye, like my handbag.
Deirdre (*staring at Cassie for a minute*) It was in a car. A blue car.
Cassie What?
Deirdre That I saw you before.
Cassie You're a lying hoor, you never saw anything.
Deirdre With a man. With him. With——

Cassie lunges at her before she can get another word out

Cassie You bastarding wee hoor! Come here till I get the skin off you!

Cassie attacks Deirdre as Nora and Marie try to pull her off

Nora Cassie!
Marie Cassie *leave* it!
Cassie I'll finish her! I will!

Deirdre shields her head and face but makes no move to defend herself. Nora and Marie manage to pull Cassie back

I'll have the tongue out of you! Then we'll see what tales you can tell!
Nora Marie, get you outside with her, I'll see to a taxi.
Marie (*trying to pull Cassie away*) Come *on* Cassie.

Cassie I'll finish her! I will!

Marie exits, dragging Cassie with her

Nora watches Deirdre as she straightens up

Nora Well your mummy didn't do much of a job with you, did she? (*Calling*) B.T., we're needing a taxi, son.

Deirdre exits

Lights change

Nora (*standing for a moment*) Oh I could say plenty I could. I've poems in my head as good as anyone. I could talk so it'd burn the wee hairs out your nose. I could. But will you tell me what the use is in talking? I've a man to see about fifteen yards of pale peach polyester mix. That's what I'm doing.

Black-out

Scene 3

Outside the Club. Moonlight

Bare wasteground

Marie and Cassie are sitting on the ground, watching the sky

Marie This is ruining my good dress, Cassie.

Cassie It is not.

Marie It is so; I can feel the damp through the back of it.

Cassie That is not ruining your best dress.

Marie So you know what my bum's feeling better than I do?

Cassie You are ruining *my* best dress that you've had on loan since Easter.

Marie Oh—well I shouldn't think you'll want it back now.

Cassie (*looking at the sky*) Will you look at that.

Marie Nearly all gone now.

Cassie Do you know what that is?

Marie (*well of course I do!*) It's an eclipse.

Cassie It's the shadow of the earth. That's our very own shadow swallowing up all the light of the moon.

Marie So where's the sun?

Cassie Australia.

Marie They won't be getting an eclipse then?

Cassie No, they'll be getting a suntan.

Marie Why did you go for that wee girl like that, Cassie?

Cassie Belfast gets an extra dark night and they get a suntan. Do you ever think there's no justice in the world at all?

Marie What did she say to you?

Cassie Well they'll all get skin cancer so we'll have the last laugh. Wet and wrinkly as feet in a bath but at least we've *got* skin.

Marie *Cassie.*

Cassie You heard what she said.

Marie I didn't hear any harm in it.

Cassie Bastarding wee hoor's been spying on me.

Marie Have you been seeing someone Cassie?

Cassie doesn't answer for a minute; she looks at Marie, hesitating, then she drops her eyes

Cassie No.

Marie Well I'm just saying I wouldn't blame you if you had Cassie, I wouldn't blame you at all.

Cassie What about the sacred bonds of marriage? What about my martyred wee Joe, pining for me in his prison cell?

Marie I'm not saying you wouldn't be doing wrong, but it's wrong that's been done to you often enough. Sure there's worse things you could be doing.

Cassie Marie Donnelly I'm surprised at you.

Marie Oh I'm just the wee prude amn't I? Cleaner than a prayer book me.

Cassie You're drunk.

Marie I am not. Just—well if you are Cassie, you need to be more careful.

Cassie If I was, Marie, you'd all know for sure. You can't keep a secret in this place. It's like trying to keep a snake in a matchbox. Oh they'll have me tarred and feathered before the week's out.

Marie Don't joke about it, Cassie.

Cassie Who's joking?

Marie I don't know how you coped with all Joe's carry on. I don't. You were the martyr there, Cassie.

Cassie It gave me peace.

Marie No but I couldn't have stood that, just the lying to you, the *lying* to you. I used to say to Michael, "If you go with someone else it'll tear the heart out of me but tell me, just tell me the truth 'cause I'd want to know, I couldn't bear not to know." He never did though. So I never worried.

Cassie No.

Marie Do you know he was like my best friend. Well, sure you're my best friend but if a man can be that kind of friend to you he was to me, could tell each other anything. That's what I miss most. The crack. The *sharing*.

Cassie Marie . . .

Marie What?

Cassie Aw Jesus I hate this place! (*She gets up, kicking the ground*)

Marie We'll get a weekend in Donegal again soon, the three of us and the kids. Sure we could all do with a break.

Cassie I'm leaving.

Marie What?

Cassie says nothing

What do you mean, you're leaving?

Cassie Do you know she gives me a tenner before every visit to go up town and buy fruit for them, "poor Martin" and "poor Joe". That's all she's allowed to give them, all she can spoil them with, fruit, so she wants them to have grapes and melons and things you've never heard of and shapes you wouldn't know how to bite into. I'll bring her home something that looks and smells like the Botanic Gardens and she'll sniff it and stroke it like it was her favourite son himself, 'stead of his dinner . . . And I'll have three four pounds safe in my pocket, saved, sure she doesn't have a clue of the price of kiwi fruit. (*Pause*) I've two hundred pounds saved. I'm going, Marie.

Marie Going where?

Cassie It's desperate, isn't it? Thirty-five years old and she's stealing from her mummy's purse. Well I thought about asking the broo for a relocation grant or something you know, but it seems to me all they can offer you is the straight swap of one hell hole for another.

Marie You talking about a holiday?

Cassie I'm talking about getting out of here.

Marie Cassie, where could you go with two kids for two hundred pounds?

Cassie says nothing for a moment

Cassie Sure you'd need thousands wouldn't you? Enough to buy yourself into a different country and a different kind of house and a different kind of life altogether. Thousands. (*Shaking her head*) But I'm going.

Marie Oh Cassie you don't mean it.

Cassie just looks at her

Marie That would kill your mummy.

Cassie I could leave her the children, Teresa turns to her before she turns to me and Brian's getting all the washing and polishing and wee cups of ice cream to keep him smiling that Martin ever got.

Marie But you couldn't leave your children. No—you couldn't leave your children.

Cassie Why not, Marie? Why not? Amn't I just a black hole of sins already? Why not?

Marie But—you *couldn't*. It'd eat you up missing them.

Cassie I'm getting chewed and swallowed and eaten alive by all that I'm wanting and can't have whatever I do. It'd be cheaper to leave them, easier . . . you're just across the road.

Marie But—Cassie.

Cassie (*sighing*) No. I can't leave the children.

Marie You wouldn't want to.

Cassie Oh Marie . . . (*Sighing*) Here's our taxi. Let's get those wains back to their own beds.

Marie and Cassie exit

Deirdre enters, looking over her shoulder

She is clutching a few bags, handbags and a carrier. She starts to empty them out, searching methodically for valuables which she pockets swiftly, pausing to try a lipstick on the back of her hand before hurling it disdainfully away. She rummages in the carrier bag, pulling out a couple of cans of beer and a knife, a switch blade. She stares at it wonderingly, then flicks out the blade. She grins. She looks back in the bag. She pulls out a swathe of material, a remnant, fifteen yards of shiny, peach polyester. Deirdre stares at it then flicks the roll so it unravels at her feet. She looks at the broad, smooth stretch of material then starts to slash at it, ripping it, trampling it till she's breathless. She stops, panting

Black-out

Scene 4

Marie's house, later that night

Cassie is slouched in a chair. Nora sits slightly more upright in another. They have fresh drinks in their hands

Cassie So the thing of it is, I wouldn't know how to do it.
Nora Where's Marie?
Cassie She's feeding the birds.
Nora What?! It's pitch black out there.
Cassie She's a flock of owls come in special.
Nora Is she all right?
Cassie Was she ever? No, she's worried she'll not be out of her bed to give the wee sparrows their crusts first thing; you wouldn't want them to go hungry would you?

Marie comes in carrying an empty plate

Nora What've you been doing Marie?
Marie Just—(*embarrassed*) I was just throwing some scraps out for the birds there.
Cassie She wouldn't tread on a spider if she found it in her shoe.
Marie (*crossing to the kitchen area*) You'll take a sandwich?
Nora If you're making one Marie, thank you, I'll be needing to get to my bed soon. What time is it?
Marie After four. (*She starts to make some sandwiches*)
Nora What a night. He promised me that remnant, it was as good as money down.
Cassie She wouldn't squash a caterpillar if she found it in her salad and here's me talking about murder.
Marie (*pausing in sandwich-making*) What?
Nora She's just talking rubbish, Marie. Months I've been planning how to make over that front room. Months.
Cassie First I thought of ground glass, but how do you grind it? Put it in a tea towel and hit it with a rolling pin, under your heel on the stone step? However you did it the bits were so big he'd never think it was gravy granules.
Nora She'd have you believing her, wouldn't she Marie?
Cassie Then I thought, stab him. Chop the vegetables, slice the bread, cut the bastard's throat—but there's a mountain of fry-ups and beer and other flab to get your knife through and who knows if he's a heart to be stabbed in at all?
Marie Pickle with your cheese, Cassie?

Cassie Thanks. So then I hit upon the perfect method: wait till he's drunk, dead drunk, blind drunk, drunk so he weeps for his mummy and wets the bed—and I wouldn't have long waiting—take a pillow, put it on his face and sit on it. It might not kill him but at least it'd stop him snoring.

Marie (*handing it to her*) Here's your sandwich.

Cassie He farts as well. Thanks.

Nora Listen to her and wasn't she desperate to marry the man?

Cassie I was desperate to marry David Essex as well. My brains hadn't grown in yet.

Nora And him with his own business and good money coming in. There's plenty would've been glad to be in your shoes, Cassie.

Cassie (*kicking her own shoes off*) They can have them, anytime they like.

Nora I don't know what you thought marriage would be, but you should've learned by your age. You've a job to do bringing up that family and making a decent home for you and your man, so get on with it.

Cassie I'll start crocheting a new house for us tomorrow.

Nora And he never lifted a finger to her, Marie. Not once.

Cassie Oh I should've thanked him for that should I? Thank you Joe for not taking the poker to me every Saturday.

Nora Well you should know what it could've been like. You of all people should've been able to see when you were well off.

Cassie What that's supposed to mean?

Marie Does anyone want some fruit loaf?

Nora As if you didn't know.

Marie I'll get some crisps out, we can have crisps with our drinks.

Cassie No, I don't know.

Nora Because you don't want to know, you never did.

Marie pauses on her way back to the kitchen, looking nervously from one to the other

Not even when you saw it with your own eyes.

Cassie doesn't say anything

I would say to him, "Would you hit your own wife in front of your own wains?" Sure I never got any answer at all but bruises. Sean was never much for conversation.

Cassie (*in a low voice*) That hardly ever happened.

Nora That happened every time he had enought drink in him.

Cassie You should've left him alone.

Nora Oh right, I shouldn't have thrown myself in the way of his fists like that.

Cassie I couldn't sleep for you nagging on and on at him, that stupid wee shrill complaining, complaining, on and on.

Nora She'd come down in the morning, Marie, and find me crying on the floor with the bruises going black on my face and all she'd say was, "Have you been upsetting my daddy again?" Go and fix herself a cup of tea.

Cassie He never beat you that bad. You'd all of us terrified with your squealing and carrying on.

Nora Eight years old, Marie, and all I saw on her face was hatred, of me. Of *me*. There's something wrong with this girl's heart.

Cassie He was the gentlest man! The gentlest man if you'd just given him peace!

Nora It was down to my Martin to stand up for his own mother; he'd come to me, crying worse than I was, "I'll get big soon mummy," he'd say, "I'll beat him back for you."

Cassie And didn't he get big enough to up and kill him! Your precious Martin put my daddy in his grave!

Nora That's a black-faced lie!

Cassie Him with his heart! He hadn't the strength left to get out of the bath himself but I never saw you lift him!

Nora I couldn't get near him for his own wee girl combing his hair and singing him songs when she should've been at the school!

Cassie He was fifty and he was an old man!

Nora It was the drink that did it to him!

Cassie And here's his own son pushing him flat on his back like he was a dog you're saying's too old to get fed any more!

Nora Sean had thrown his dinner at me!

Cassie He missed!

Nora He would have killed me if he could!

Marie You'll wake the children.

Nora and Cassie fall silent

Marie goes to the kitchen area, opens some crisps, puts them in a bowl, brings them out and sets them down

Nora and Cassie stare at their drinks

Cassie I never hated you.

Nora scrubs one fierce hand over her eyes but gives no sign she's heard

I just wanted you to make it happen different.

Nora Well you'll need to go to some other place where they make the world different, Cassie.

Cassie Well so I will.

Nora You do that.

Cassie I will. I'm leaving.

Nora Though it seems to me there's not a place in the world that is different.

Cassie Well I'll write and tell you.

Nora Oh she's got her flight booked, Marie.

Cassie Tell her, Marie.

Marie It's not for me to tell her, Cassie.

Cassie Mummy, I've two hundred pounds saved and I'm getting out.

Nora Oh.

No one says anything else for a second

So you've got yourself a flat?

Cassie No. I'm leaving Belfast.
Nora What?
Cassie I'm getting on a ferry and I'm getting out.
Nora What are you saying to me, Cassie?
Cassie How many ways do you want me to say it!

There is a pause

Nora Well, where are you going?
Cassie I'll see where I get to. I'm telling you though I'm not going to be one of those that go out on one boat and come home on the next with their luck all spent. I'm leaving, Mummy.
Nora And what about your children?
Cassie They'll be better off out of here.
Nora Are you going to just tear them out by the roots and drag them along after you?
Cassie No . . . I . . .
Nora To live God knows where on two hundred pound?
Cassie I'll send for them . . . (*Catching Marie's eye*) Oh don't look at me Marie.
Nora Oh don't come it with your tall tales again, Cassie. Two hundred pounds indeed.
Cassie Oh is it proof you're wanting? Here then. (*She gets up and goes to Michael's picture*)
Marie Cassie what are you doing?

Cassie feels behind it, stops then starts running her hand frantically over the back of the picture

What are you doing to Michael!?

Cassie pulls it off the wall and looks at the back of it. She stares at it for a minute then turns to Marie

Cassie Where is it?
Marie What?
Cassie My money. Where'd you put it Marie?
Marie I never touched a penny of yours, Cassie!
Cassie You were the only one knew I had it.
Marie I never knew you'd hidden it up the back of Michael!
Cassie I had to put it through here; have you seen the way she dusts? (*She points at Nora*)
Marie Well I never touched your money, Cassie.
Cassie Oh Jesus, someone's lifted it. (*She collapses back into her chair, still clutching Michael's picture*) They've taken my money off me! (*She bows her head. She seems about to cry*)

Nora and Marie look at each other

Nora (*crossing to her*) Cassie?

Cassie shakes her head

(Hesitating a moment) Och you're not crying, are you?

Cassie just looks at her

Well, what age are you to be making up daydreams and spoiling your face crying for them. Come on, now.

Nora pats briskly at Cassie's shoulder

Cassie knocks Nora's hand away

Well you're not going anywhere, Cassie Ryan. That's clear as daylight.
Cassie *(quietly)* I'm going anyway, money or no money.
Nora But your home's here! Your family's here!
Cassie Yes. It is.

Cassie and Nora stare at each other for a few seconds

Nora And what I feel goes for nothing, does it?
Cassie What do you feel, Mummy? For me? What have you got left?

Nora turns away from her shaking

Marie takes a step towards her but before she can get there Nora turns, struggling to look bright

Nora Well—thanks for the sandwich Marie, but we'll not be troubling you further; you must be desperate for your bed.
Cassie *(still staring at Nora)* Can I get another drink, Marie?

Marie hesitates again, looking between them

Nora *(pleading)* Cassie . . .
Cassie Good-night, Mummy. *(She looks away from Nora)*
Nora *(drawing herself up)* Oh you'll be telling me a different tale in the morning! There's no end to your wild tales, Cassie! There's no end to them, Marie! *(She snatches up her drink and takes an angry gulp)* And I'd it all to do. I'd it all to put up with! Are you hearing me?

Cassie doesn't look at Nora

(Taking another gulp) He's lost my remnant, Marie. He's lost it. I'd all the money saved, as good as paid. It's gone he says, gone. I'll never find a colour like that again. Months I'd been dreaming of the glow that would give my front room. Months. And he's lost it. I'll never have it the way I want it now. Never. *(She is getting tearful in her turn)* My lovely wee room. It could be lovely, couldn't it, Marie?
Marie You'll get it right, Nora.
Nora Well where will I ever find a colour like that again? Tell me that? *(Waiting for a response)* Cassie? I'm asking you!
Cassie *(looking up at Nora)* Good night, Mummy.

Nora stares at her for a moment, then she nods

Nora Well I'm going up the town tomorrow. I'm just going to go up the town and buy a piece of what I want. I'll get credit. I'll give them a false

address and I'll get credit and I'll have my loose covers. And if you don't
want to come and help choose them, Cassie, you needn't sit on them.

Nora exits

*Marie puts the gin bottle down in front of Cassie. Cassie helps herself to
another drink*

Marie (*quietly*) It'll tear the heart out of her, Cassie.
Cassie Mummy's heart is made of steel. She had to grow it that way.

*Marie reaches over and takes Michael's picture. She goes and rehangs it
carefully*

There's a waitress up that club will be walking round without her hair
tomorrow if I can find her.
Marie You don't know it was her. There's people in and out of here all the
time.
Cassie Who else would it be?
Marie Well—if she's thieving round the club there'll be others sort her out
before you do. (*She steps back to admire the picture*)
Cassie How do you stand it here. Marie?
Marie Sure where else would I go?
Cassie How do you keep that smile on your face?
Marie Super-glue.
Cassie There's not one piece of bitterness in you, is there?
Marie Oh Cassie.
Cassie You see, you're good. And I'm just wicked.
Marie Aye you're a bold woman altogether.
Cassie Is it hard being good?
Marie I took lessons.
Cassie Well, tell me what you've got to smile about Marie, because I'm sure
I can't see it.
Marie I've a lot to be thankful of. I've my kids, a job, a nice wee house and I
can still pay for it.
Cassie You've two wee boys growing out of their clothes faster than you
can get them new ones, a part-time job licking envelopes for a wage that
wouldn't keep a budgie and three red bills on your mantelpiece there.
Marie That's what's great about a Saturday out with you Cassie, you just
know how to look at the bright side of things, don't you?
Cassie Well just tell me how you can keep filling that kettle and making folk
tea without pouring it over their head?
Marie Ah well you see, I'm a mug.
Cassie I think you are.
Marie I didn't marry Joe, but . . .
Cassie No. You did not. That mug was me.
Marie See Cassie, I've had better times with Michael than a lot of women
get in their whole lives with a man.
Cassie And that keeps you going?
Marie It's a warming kind of thought.

Cassie holds out her arms to Michael's pictures

Cassie (*singing*) "Thanks—for the memories."

Marie Oh Cassie.

Cassie That doesn't work, Marie. I've tried to keep myself warm that way. Find some man with good hands and a warm skin and wrap him round you to keep the rain off; you'll be damp in the end anyway.

Marie Cassie, don't talk like that; you know you've not done half the wild things you make out.

Cassie Not a quarter of what I've wanted to Marie, but enough to know it doesn't work. Grabbing onto some man because he smells like excitement, he smells like escape. They can't take you anywhere except into the back seat of their car. They're all the same.

Marie If that's what you think of them that'll be all you'll find.

Cassie gets up to stand, looking at Michael

Cassie They are *all* the same, Marie.

Marie No.

Cassie *No*, not *Michael*. (*Sarcastically*) Wasn't he just the perfect man, the perfect saint of a man.

Marie He was no saint.

Cassie He was not.

Marie I never said he was a saint.

Cassie Not much perfect about him.

Marie We cared about each other! We were honest with each other!

Cassie Honest!?

Marie We were. He was a good man!

Cassie Good!? He was a lying worm like every one of them!

There is a pause

Marie I think you should go home, Cassie.

Cassie So he told you all about it did he? All the times he made a fool of you to your face?

Marie Just go now.

Cassie I don't believe you could have kept that smile on your face Marie, not if he was honestly telling you what he was up to.

Marie Cassie . . .

Cassie Making a fool of you with all those women.

There is a pause

Marie I heard the stories. Of course I heard them.

Cassie Did you, though?

Marie He was a great-looking man. He was away a lot. There were bound to be stories.

Cassie There were books of them, Marie.

Marie But if there'd been any truth in them Michael would've told me himself.

Cassie Oh *Marie*!

Marie That's trust Cassie!

Cassie That's *stupidity*, Marie. You haven't the sense of a hen with its head off!

Marie Michael would no more lie to me than you would, Cassie.

Cassie Well we both did! That's what I'm telling you Marie! We were both lying to you for years!

Marie freezes where she is

Ah Jesus . . . (*She moves to take another swig of her drink*)

Marie doesn't move throughout the following

(*She can't look at Marie*) He started it but I followed it through. That was before Joe was lifted. Even the smell of *him* was bringing my dinner up on me. I felt like I was trapped in this little black box and it was falling in on me. Michael was a window. Just a bit of excitement you know? He was exciting, Michael . . . Marie? I'm going to tell you this, Marie. I'm tired of keeping it from you. I'm tired of keeping the smile on your face. I knew it was bad. I knew lying to you was worse. I wanted to tell you . . . but I've been telling you for four years and you wouldn't hear me. Are you hearing me now Marie? We'd just go out in his car, that old blue one you had before my daddy won it. Sometimes we wouldn't do anything you know? Just sit. Talk. He was great crack, Michael. (*Pause*) I didn't think it was so bad. I always knew he loved you. He always loved you, Marie. And he did always tell you the truth, but there's only so much of the truth anyone wants to hear. That's what he gave you Marie, what he gave everyone, enough of the truth to keep us all charmed.

Marie has still not moved, her eyes fixed on Cassie's face

So. There you are. That's the truth. Now you can tear the face off me.

Still nothing

Marie.

No response

(*Sighing*) I'll put the kettle on.

Marie (*whispering*) Get out.

Cassie stops

GET OUT OF MY HOUSE!

Cassie hesitates, she takes a step towards Marie. Marie steps back

Cassie (*urgently*) Well, what did you expect? Sure what man would tell you that kind of truth? He'd be crazy to talk about it. What woman would stand for that? If he told you, he'd have to change. They'd sooner leave than they would change, Marie . . . You didn't want him to leave.

There is a pause. Marie just stares at Cassie

Marie (*whispering*) Hell isn't deep enough for you, Cassie Ryan.

Cassie flinches. She turns to pick her coat up

Cassie Sure we'll—we'll talk about it another time.
Marie No.
Cassie We're both thinking through drink tonight but . . .

Marie grabs crisps, drinks, everything she can lay hands on. She pelts Cassie with them, moving closer and closer

   (*Trying frantically to protect herself*) Jesus! Jesus, Marie! No!

Marie is on top of her, a heavy plate raised to smash down

Cassie stares up at her, terrified

Marie lowers her arm

Marie (*turning away*) Just get out.

   Cassie straightens up, shaking, and edges out the door

Marie stands for another frozen moment then she screams, a great howl of pain and loss

A child starts to cry off stage

Marie lowers her head, hugging herself, rocking herself

The child goes on crying

After a moment Marie raises her head

   (*Eyes, shut, still rocking*) Your daddy was a good man and a brave man and he did the best he could and he's in heaven watching out for you . . . And that's what keeps us all together, keeps me going, keeps me . . . (*She can't go on. After a second she gets up and goes to the child*)

   Marie exits

   Deirdre enters and goes and sits in the chair Cassie has vacated. She is still wearing her waitressing clothes but her face is bare of make-up, her hair limp again. She is nursing one arm as if it hurts her. She sits looking up at Michael. She takes out the knife and flicks out the blade. Experimentally she pushes it into the back of the chair. She tries another couple of slow stabs then leaves the knife there, its handle sticking out. She pushes at it, pushing it further in, wiggling the blade, her expression intent

Off stage the crying stops

   After a moment Marie enters

She stops dead when she sees Deirdre. Deirdre turns quickly, leaving the knife where it is

Marie What do you want?
Deirdre I brought your money back. (*She pulls Cassie's roll of bills out of her pocket and lays it on the table*) There's a fiver gone on chips and drinks.

Marie comes further into the room, watching Deirdre like she's a dog deciding whether to bite or not

Marie What happened to your arm?
Deirdre Just these fellas up the club. They wanted me to go in their car. It's just bruised.

Marie looks at her for a moment

Marie You've followed me, you've watched me and you've stolen from me
Deirdre Yeah.
Marie What more do you want?

Deirdre points to the picture of Michael

Deirdre Him.

Marie crosses slowly to look at Michael then she rips him off the wall and throws the picture at Deirdre

Marie Take him.

Deirdre clutches the picture awkwardly. Bemused

What good do you think he'll be to you?
Deirdre He was my daddy.
Marie What?
Deirdre He was. He was my daddy.

Marie closes her eyes for a moment

Marie Why do you think he was?
Deirdre My mum told me.
Marie Oh. (*She opens her eyes and looks at Michael*)
Deirdre She said my dad was a bad man, and for years I thought my daddy was a hood, then she told me he was a bad man because he left her, left her flat with me on the way and I thought that didn't make him so bad because didn't I want to leave her too? So I started asking. (*Pause*) No one will tell you the truth to your face. But I heard his name, so I went looking for him.
Marie And did you find him?
Deirdre I used to follow him about. That's how I saw him with her.
Marie Cassie.
Deirdre Aye.
Marie You saw them together?
Deirdre In his car. She was wearing a bright red dress with no back to it, that made me stare first you know because I couldn't imagine how she could stand it being so cold, even in his car. Then they moved and I saw his face so I had to stay then, I had to stay and watch. I saw his face and I saw hers just before he kissed her . . . Just before he did she looked like my Granny, old and tired and like she didn't care about anything at all anymore . . . (*Pause*) I stopped following him after that. I thought if he was with her he'd never come back to me and my mum. Then I heard he was dead . . . (*Pause*) I didn't know where to look for him then. I'm cold.

50 Bold Girls

Marie doesn't respond

Can I get a cup of tea or something?
Marie No.
Deirdre Oh. (*She looks at Michael, then puts him down*) That's just a picture.
Marie Yes.
Deirdre I thought—you know—I thought if I came and watched—maybe I wouldn't lose him altogether.
Marie And was he still here?
Deirdre No. But I kept looking. (*Pause*) Now I've told you everything. Now you've to tell me.
Marie You can ask anyone. They all know stories about Michael. There's no end to the stories about Michael.
Deirdre But you know the truth.
Marie Oh, it's truth you're wanting?
Deirdre They said he was with the Provos.
Marie He was wild when he was young.
Deirdre They said he was a hero?
Marie Maybe he was.
Deirdre What did he do?
Marie He went away to do it. I stayed here and cleaned the floor and when he came in I'd put his tea in front of him. Do you want to know what he had for his tea? I could tell you that.

Deirdre doesn't move

Deirdre I brought your money back. So you've to tell me.
Marie But I've no story, haven't they told you? I know nothing at all. That's the only story I'm fit to tell you, about nothing at all ... Except being brave and coping great and never complaining and holding the home together ... Is that the story you're wanting?

Deirdre says nothing

Oh but they think I don't know how to be bitter, they think I never learned. I'm just a wee girl with a smile that feeds the birds. (*Pause*) So is this the truth you wanted to rob me of? Is this what you wanted to hear? Go you back now, go you back to your own mother. She can tell you how bad he was, how he lied to her; that's a better story, that's a story that'll keep you safe from any man with a gentle smile and warm hands. Go you back to your own place!
Deirdre She'll have locked me out.
Marie So go back to the street. (*She turns away*)

Deirdre doesn't stir

Deirdre (*quietly*) She's not sure. She's never been sure, if he was.
Marie So he only cheated on me with the best, well, that's a great comfort to me isn't it? Have you been chasing a herd of daddies then?
Deirdre But you'd know. I know you'd look at me and you'd be sure.

Marie doesn't turn

Deirdre gets up and clumsily pulls off her top, drags off the jeans. There are bruises all over her back. She goes to Marie and pushes the clothes in front of her

Here, that's you got everything back.

Marie turns, startled, then starts to laugh, hysterically. Deirdre hurls the clothes at her. She snatches the knife out of the chair and waves the blade at Marie. She advances on her slowly

I want the truth out of you. I mean it.

Marie backs off a step

Tell me!

Suddenly Marie flies at her

Marie Tell you! I'll tell you!

She wrenches the knife and the picture off the startled Deirdre and smashes and slashes Michael's picture with swift, efficient destructiveness. She looks down at the pieces at her feet for a long moment. She drops the knife on top of them. Her breathing slows. She goes to the kitchen area and comes back with a half-filled rubbish sack and some newspaper. She kneels down and starts to clear up the pieces of the picture

(*Quietly*) Watch your feet on that glass there. (*She wraps the glass and the shredded picture in newspaper. She wraps the knife as well. She drops both in the rubbish sack and takes it back to the kitchen*)

Deirdre has barely moved through all of this, she watches Marie tearfully

Marie returns from the kitchen, wiping her hands

(*Still quietly*) There. (*She looks at Deirdre*) Those are some bruises you've got.

Marie reaches out and touches Deirdre's shoulder

Deirdre flinches, then allows the touch

Marie turns her gently. She looks at her bruised body. Marie touches Deirdre's back

Marie Who did this to you?
Deirdre Just the fella she's got living with her just now.
Marie (*stroking Deirdre's back*) They took the lying head off Michael, didn't you know? Didn't they tell you that story?
Deirdre (*quietly*) Yes. (*She pulls away from Marie*)

Marie seems to focus on her again

Marie Ah God forgive me . . . (*She sways momentarily. She runs her hands over her face*) You should go home. It's late.

Deirdre doesn't move

Here. (*She offers the clothes again*)

Deirdre shakes her head again

Marie takes a blanket off the back of the sofa and drapes it over her

Well whoever your daddy was, it's a pity he didn't give you the sense to look after yourself. Are you hungry just now?

Deirdre shakes her head

Marie goes and sits closer to her

(*Gentler*) The thing about daddys, all the daddys, is they up and leave you; they go out with their friends, they go inside, they die, they leave you. You'll always have it all to do so there's no good wishing on them. (*Pause*) Half the time I don't think they want to go. Sure half the time all they want to do is something better for us all, for them, for us. They don't want to be raging and screaming and hurting more than they can ever forget in the booze or the crack or the men beating men. I don't think they know what they want at all or how to get it if they did. So they leave and we've it all to do but we're missing each other even when we're together and so it goes on and so it goes on and so it always will go on, till we learn some way to change—because this place is no different to anywhere else. (*Pause*) I never told him that. It wasn't that I lied. I just didn't tell all the truth that was in me. Sure, what good would telling that kind of truth do you? You'd be crazy to talk about it wouldn't you? What man would listen to that? If he heard you he'd have to change. Maybe he'd sooner leave. I didn't want him to leave. I loved him. I can't throw that away even now. I loved him. You see I'm just a mug, Deirdre. Cassie was right. I knew who you were the first time I saw you. I knew. (*Pause*) What age are you?

Deirdre I'm sixteen.

Marie (*sucking in her breath*) I was married sixteen years.

Deirdre I know.

There is a pause

Marie Sometimes—sometimes when he came home he'd cry, from tiredness, because his heart was sick in him. He'd cry and I'd comfort him.

Deirdre pushes at the money on the table for a minute

Deirdre I'll get the other fiver to you.

Marie It doesn't matter.

Deirdre It's your money.

Marie It's Cassie's now. It'll go back to her. She needs it to dream with. (*She shakes her head*) She'll not use it for much else. You're shivering.

Deirdre I've cold blood. That's what they say . . . I'm away now. (*She gets up*)

Marie You can't go out like that.

Deirdre pulls the blanket round her; she looks at Marie

Your daddy ... Your daddy was a man, like any other. If he knew you
were alive he never told me. And he's dead now ... You've got his eyes.

They look at each other for a minute

Deirdre nods

Deirdre I'll be away up the road then.
Marie Not at this hour, it's nearly morning. I'll get the breakfast started.
Come on you'll be hungry soon. (*She moves back to the kitchen and starts
getting out food*) You can give me a hand if you like.

Deirdre hesitates, then goes to join her·

(*Handing her a loaf*) Slice the top crust off that bread but keep it.
Deirdre What for?
Marie For the birds. Did you ever feed the birds, Deirdre?
Deirdre No.
Marie I like the common wee birds, the pigeons and the starlings and the
sparrows, it's easy enough to build a great wee nest when you've a whole
forest to fly in, but you'd need to be something special to build one round
the Falls. Someone should feed them. (*Pause*) You make crumbs of that.
I'll put the kettle on.

Lights fade to Black-out

FURNITURE AND PROPERTY LIST

On stage: Iron
Ironing board
Pile of crumpled clothes
Socks
Pegs
Damp sheets and towels
Broken toys
Cardboard boxes. *In them*: toys
New and gleaming toys with flashing lights
Teabags and milk
Mugs
Pots and pans
Cutlery and crockery
Cooker. *On it:* kettle on the boil, cooked food
Armchairs bald with age
Sofa. *On it:* blanket
Coal fire with a gleaming hearth
Small picture of the Virgin on the wall
Large grainy blow-up photo of a young man framed in glass
Sink
Table *On it:* potatoes, potato peeler, bread and matches
Mop
TV
Blind at the window
Radio

Off stage: Four packets of crisps, two packets of Silk Cut, packet of chocolate
biscuits **(Marie)**
Pile of damp sheets **(Nora)**
Plastic cup of red syrup **(Cassie)**
Fabric sample and towel **(Nora)**
Wet mop, soggy packet of cigarettes **(Cassie)**
Jewellery **(Deirdre)**

Personal: **Cassie:** wad of money
Marie: watch

Scene 2

Strike: Previous set

Set: Battered and cheap tables and chairs
Small stand like a lectern. *On it:* sheets of paper and pen

Rotating fans
Glitterballs

Off stage: Tray. *On it:* six drinks **(Marie)**
Large box **(Deirdre)**

Personal: **Cassie:** bag. *In it:* purse. *In it:* tickets, five pound notes
Marie: bag. *In it:* purse. *In it:* tickets, five pound notes
Nora: bag. *In it:* purse. *In it:* tickets, five pound notes

SCENE 3

Strike: Previous set

Off stage: Bags. In one: couple of cans of beer, knife with a switch blade, fifteen
yards of shiny, peach polyester. Handbags. *In them:* purses etc. *In one:*
lipstick **(Deirdre)**

Personal: **Cassie:** bag
Marie: bag

SCENE 4

Strike: Previous set

Set: Furniture and property used in Act 1, Scene 1, apart from potatoes,
potato peeler, dirty crockery and kettle on the boil
Bottle of gin
Lemonade
Half-filled rubbish sack
Newspapers
Crisps, margarine and pot of pickle
Coat on chair
Drinks

Off stage: Empty plate **(Marie)**

Personal: **Deirdre:** knife with a switch blade and roll of money

LIGHTING PLOT

Two interior settings. One exterior. Practical fittings required: glitterball for Scene 2

SCENE 1

To open: Darkness except for light on **Deirdre**

Cue 1	**Deirdre:** "... and the helicopter overhead." *Black-out; after a few moments bring up interior lighting*	(Page 1)
Cue 2	**Marie:** "There'll maybe be something in a minute." *Cross-fade to spotlight on* **Deirdre**	(Page 8)
Cue 3	**Deirdre:** "Can't keep me out." *Fade light on* **Deirdre**. *Light up on* **Marie**	(Page 8)
Cue 4	**Marie:** "Well—I was just seventeen after all." *Revert to general interior lighting*	(Page 9)
Cue 5	**Marie** switches on television *TV flicker effect*	(Page 12)
Cue 6	**Marie** switches off the television *Cut flicker effect*	(Page 16)
Cue 7	**Cassie** move to the radio *Lighting change*	(Page 16)
Cue 8	**Deirdre:** "... and point where you liked." *Lighting change*	(Page 16)
Cue 9	**Marie** moves over to put the television back on *Flicker effect*	(Page 16)
Cue 10	**Cassie** moves out of the acting area *Lighting change*	(Page 20)
Cue 11	**Cassie:** "... me that lied to him." *Revert to previous lighting*	(Page 21)
Cue 12	**Deirdre** exits *Black-out*	(Page 22)

SCENE 2

To open: Dim lighting with glitterballs and spots

Cue 13	**Marie** and **Nora** sit down *Lighting change*	(Page 29)
Cue 14	**Cassie:** "... that's why they hurt you so much." *Return to previous lighting*	(Page 29)

EFFECTS PLOT

Cue 1   **Marie:** "I think you're maybe right."   (Page 7)
         Sound of a distant explosion

Cue 2   **Marie:** "Cassie, that can't be healthy at all—"   (Page 10)
         Sound of a few gunshots, close at hand

Cue 3   **Marie** switches on the television   (Page 12)
         Sound of TV programme

Cue 4   **Nora** turns the sound up   (Page 12)
         Increase TV volume

Cue 5   **Deirdre** takes the plate without comment   (Page 13)
         Another shot, more distant

Cue 6   **Nora** turns the sound up   (Page 14)
         Increase TV volume

Cue 7   **Marie** switches off the television   (Page 16)
         Cut sound

Cue 8   **Marie** moves over to put the television back on   (Page 16)
         Sound of early weekend evening programmes

Cue 9   **Cassie:** "Can I get off my feet?   (Page 23)
         Sudden burst of music and buzz of talk (fade after a while)

Cue 10   **Deirdre** walks to Marie   (Page 29)
         Ragged applause

Cue 11   Lights revert to normal   (Page 30)
         Dance music plays in the background

Cue 12   **Marie** screams, a great howl of pain and loss   (Page 48)
         A child starts to cry off stage

Cue 13   **Deirdre** wiggles the blade in the chair   (Page 48)
         Crying stops

MADE AND PRINTED IN GREAT BRITAIN BY
LATIMER TREND & COMPANY LTD PLYMOUTH
MADE IN ENGLAND